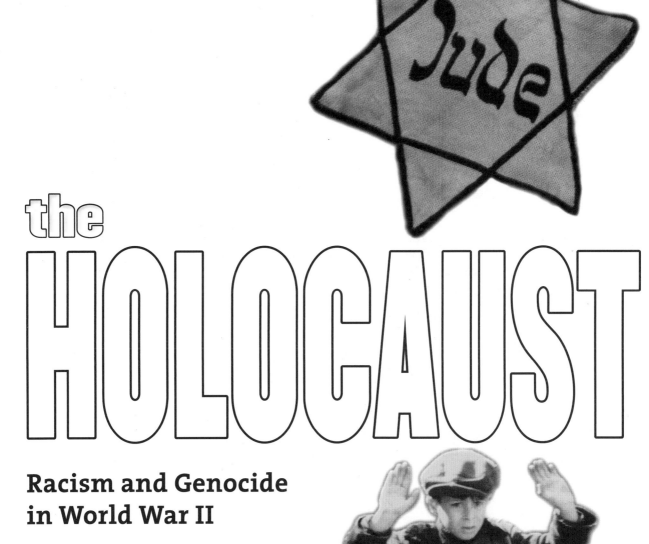

# the HOLOCAUST

## Racism and Genocide in World War II

**Carla Mooney**
Illustrated by Tom Casteel

Nomad Press
A division of Nomad Communications
10 9 8 7 6 5 4 3 2 1

This book was manufactured by Marquis Book Printing,
Montmagny, Québec, Canada
April 2017, Job #136232
ISBN Softcover: 978-1-61930-510-6
ISBN Hardcover: 978-1-61930-506-9

Educational Consultant, Marla Conn

Questions regarding the ordering of this book should be addressed to
Nomad Press
2456 Christian St.
White River Junction, VT 05001
www.nomadpress.net

Printed in Canada.

# More Social Studies titles in the **Inquire and Investigate** series

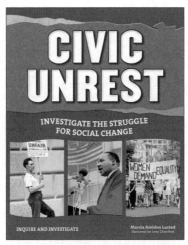

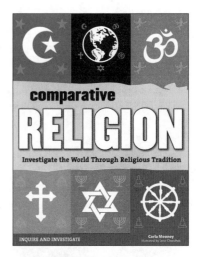

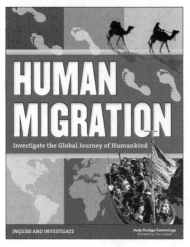

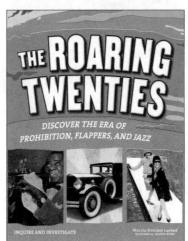

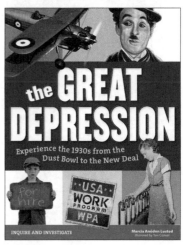

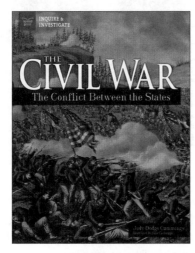

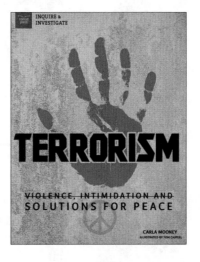

Interested in primary sources?

**PS**

**Look for this icon.**

You can use a smartphone or tablet app to scan the QR codes and explore more! Cover up neighboring QR codes to make sure you're scanning the right one. You can find a list of URLs on the Resources page.

If the QR code doesn't work, try searching the Internet with the Keyword Prompts to find other helpful sources.

🔍 Holocaust

# Contents

# TIMELINE

1918 ........................ After Germany's defeat in World War I, Kaiser Wilhelm II abdicates and flees the country. The Weimar Republic leads Germany.

1919 ........................ The Treaty of Versailles forces Germany to accept responsibility and pay reparations for World War I.

1920 ........................ A rising Nazi Party star named Adolf Hitler presents a 25-point plan at a Nazi Party meeting.

1923 ........................ Hitler and the Nazi Party unsuccessfully attempt to overthrow the Weimar Republic, an event that would become known as the Beer Hall Putsch.

1925 ........................ After his release from prison, Adolf Hitler becomes the leader of the Nazi Party.

January 1933 .......... President Paul von Hindenburg appoints Adolf Hitler chancellor of Germany.

March 1933 ............ The Schutzstaffel, or SS, paramilitary organization opens Dachau concentration camp outside of Munich, Germany.

April 1933 .............. The Nazi Party calls for the boycott of Jewish-owned shops and businesses in Germany.

1933 ........................ Beginning in 1933, the Germans pass more than 400 decrees and regulations that restrict the public and private lives of the Jewish people.

1935 .................. Germany passes the Nuremberg Race Laws, which exclude Jews from being German citizens and prohibit them from marrying a person with German blood.

March 1938 ........... Germany annexes Austria.

November 1938 ..... Kristallnacht is a violent two nights of attacks on Jewish people and businesses throughout Germany and its territories.

September 1939 ..... Germany invades Poland, triggering the start of World War II.

October 1939 ........ The Germans establish a ghetto in Piotrków Trybunalski, Poland.

May 1940 ............... Germany attacks France.

July 1940 ............... The Battle of Britain begins as the British and German air forces battle for air superiority.

October 1940 ........ The Nazis open the Warsaw Ghetto.

September 1941 ..... Mobile killing units shoot about 34,000 Jews at Babi Yar, outside Kiev, Ukraine.

December 1941 ...... Japan bombs Pearl Harbor and the United States enters the war.

December 1941 ...... The first killing operations begin at Chelmno in occupied Poland.

# TIMELINE

**January 1942** ......... Germans begin the mass deportation of more than 65,000 Jews from Lodz to the Chelmno killing center.

**January 1942** ......... The Wannsee Conference is held near Berlin, Germany, to discuss the Final Solution.

**1942** ..................... The Germans start mass deportations of Jews from Europe's ghettos to concentration camps and killing centers.

**April 1943** ............. Jewish resistance fights back against the Nazis in the Warsaw Ghetto uprising.

**October 1943** ......... The Danish people evacuate their Jewish citizens before the Nazis are able to deport them.

**June 1944** .............. Allied forces invade Normandy, France, on D-Day.

**June 1944** .............. The Soviets launch an offensive in the east against Nazi forces.

**August 1944** .......... The Allies liberate Paris, France.

**January 1945** ......... Thousands of concentration camp prisoners are forced on death marches to empty the camps before Allied forces arrive.

**January 1945** ......... Soviet troops liberate Auschwitz-Birkenau concentration camp in Poland.

**April 1945**............... Allied forces surround Berlin.

**April 1945**............... American troops liberate Dachau concentration camp.

**April 1945**............... Adolf Hitler commits suicide.

**May 1945**................ Theresienstadt in Czechoslovakia is the last death camp to be liberated.

**May 1945**................ Germany surrenders.

**November 1945**...... The Nuremberg trials of leading German officials for war crimes opens before the International Military Tribunal.

**1948**......................... The U.S. Congress passes the Displaced Persons Act, which provides immigration visas for about 400,000 people between 1949 and 1952.

**1948**......................... The State of Israel is established. It is the first Jewish state in 2,000 years.

**1948**......................... The United Nations adopts the Universal Declaration of Human Rights, which lists, for the first time, the fundamental human rights that are to be universally protected.

**1953**......................... The last Jewish displaced persons camp in Germany closes.

**2005**......................... The United Nations marks January 27th as International Holocaust Remembrance Day, on the anniversary of the liberation of Auschwitz-Birkenau concentration camp by the Soviet army in 1945.

WAR CRIME
DISCRIMINATION
RESISTANCE
PROPAGANDA
AXIS
ATROCITY
ALLIES
SA
TREATY
HOLOCAUST
ANTI-SEMITISM
JUDAISM
ARMISTICE
DEMOCRACY
JUSTICE
RIGHTS
ROMANI
BRUTALITY
INTOLERANCE
IMMIGRANT
CRIMES AGAINST HUMANITY
TREATY OF VERSAILLES
DESPOTISM
GESTAPO
SS
PERSECUTION
NUREMBERG LAWS
NAZI
MASS MURDER
TREASON
FRONT
OPPRESS
EYEWITNESS
TOLERANCE
GHETTO
CITIZEN
HYGIENE
RACISM
PREJUDICE
GENOCIDE
ARYAN
MORALITY
IMMIGRATION
DEPORT
CIVIL RIGHTS
HUMAN RIGHTS
CONCENTRATION CAMP
KINDERTRANSPORT
POGROM
COMMEMORATION
CHANCELLOR
GAS CHAMBER
PARTISAN
CREMATORIA
ZEGOTA
EXILE
BOYCOTT
SWASTIKA
ENABLING ACT
DICTATORSHIP
COLLABORATE
ALLIANCE
RESILIENCE
IDEOLOGY

# What Was the Holocaust?

Why is it important to study the Holocaust?

There are many reasons people study the Holocaust, including learning more about ourselves as a people and developing ways to prevent genocide from happening again.

The Holocaust is a grim moment in human history that evolved slowly, from 1933 to 1945. It began with discrimination and ended in mass murder. The Holocaust was the systematic, state-sponsored persecution and murder of Jews by the Nazi regime.

More than 6 million Jewish people were killed in the pogroms and concentration camps of Germany. This was nearly two out of every three Jews living in Europe at the time.

Countless more people, including the mentally ill, disabled, and a group called the Romani, also suffered at the hands of the Nazi Party.

The Nazis believed that Germans were racially superior and they were determined to destroy those who threatened their so-called "pure" race. They also murdered political opponents, homosexuals, and prisoners of war. Between 2 and 3 million prisoners of war from the Soviet Union were killed or died of starvation, disease, or neglect at the hands of their Nazi captors.

Although the Holocaust ended in 1945, its lasting effects are still felt around the world today. The Holocaust was not an accident in history—it occurred because individuals, organizations, and governments made choices. These choices legalized discrimination and allowed prejudice, hatred, and ultimately mass murder.

The study of the Holocaust has different meanings for different individuals, but it is imperative that everyone has a deep awareness and appreciation of this tumultuous time in history. It teaches us critical lessons in morality, human behavior, and what it means to be responsible citizens. The Holocaust serves to remind us that democratic institutions and values are not automatically sustained, but need to be appreciated, nurtured, and protected.

# ONE PERSON'S PERSPECTIVE

We can see how the rise of Nazi Germany was perceived by people around the world when we look at the experiences of one man—William E. Dodd. On July 5, 1933, Dodd, along with his wife, Martha, and his son and daughter, boarded the *Washington*, a ship sailing from the United States to Hamburg, Germany. Dodd was to become the next American ambassador to Germany.

A professor at the University of Chicago and a leading historian of the American South, Dodd was an unlikely choice for the job. However, President Franklin D. Roosevelt believed that Dodd was suited for the job. He wanted Dodd to be a standing example of democracy in Germany during a time when whispers circulated about the Nazi persecution of Jews and the country's increasing suspension of democracy.

## PRIMARY SOURCES

Primary sources come from people who were eyewitnesses to events. They might write about the event, take pictures, post short messages to social media or blogs, or record the event for radio or video. Why are primary sources important? Do you learn differently from primary sources than from secondary sources, which come from people who did not directly experience the event?

**PS**

## BEAR WITNESS ✡

At least five men turned down the ambassador post in Germany before William E. Dodd accepted the position.

When the Dodds sailed for Germany, a man named Adolf Hitler had been Germany's chancellor for six months. Newspapers in America and around the world reported stories about Hitler's rise and the German government's increasingly hostile attitude and brutal treatment of Jews, communists, and other opponents. Many people believed that the reports of Germany's transformation from a modern democracy into a brutal dictatorship were exaggerated.

When Dodd first arrived in Berlin, he, too, thought that the warnings about the troubles in Germany were overstated. He was convinced that moderate opinions in the government would prevail and that the mistreatment of the Jewish people would lessen. Dodd believed that the best approach was to encourage more humane treatment of the Jews through private conversations with moderates in Hitler's government.

> Even after he met Hitler in 1933, Dodd remained steadfast in his belief that Hitler and his top men would make reasonable choices.

## RUMBLES OF VIOLENCE

By 1934, Dodd began to suspect that he was wrong. During a meeting between Dodd and Hitler in 1934, Hitler condemned all Jews and blamed them for the bad feelings that had arisen in America and other countries against the Germans. When Dodd suggested a more peaceful and humane treatment of Jewish people in Germany, Hitler dismissed it. He claimed that the Jews intended to ruin his country.

> Hitler promised that if the Jews
> continued their activity in Germany,
> he would bring a complete end
> of all of them in his country.

Nazi violence was committed against individual Jewish people, American visitors to Germany, and others who disagreed with Hitler and the Nazis. Through these cases, Dodd came face-to-face with Nazi brutality. In one incident, an American radio commentator named H.V. Kaltenborn and his family were attacked during a vacation in Germany when they did not salute a parade of the German army.

## VOCAB LAB

There is a lot of new vocabulary in this book. Turn to the glossary in the back when you come to a word you don't understand. Practice your new vocabulary in the **VOCAB LAB** activities in each chapter.

Adolf Hitler salutes a parade of stormtroopers in 1935.

photo credit: Charles Russell, National Archives

From June 30 to July 2, 1934, Adolf Hitler, the chancellor of Germany and leader of the Nazi Party, ordered the murder of several leaders of the Sturmabteilung, also known as the stormtroopers, or SA. Led by Ernst Röhm, the SA numbered nearly 3 million men by 1934. They outnumbered the German Army, which was limited to 100,000 men. Many of Germany's leaders were afraid that the SA was growing too powerful.

On June 28, Hitler ordered Röhm to gather top SA leaders at a Bavarian spa. Bodyguards for the Nazi Party leaders, called the Schutzstaffel, or SS, surprised the SA leaders and took them to prison, where most of them were shot. Nazi leaders also killed other political enemies. Hitler was free to declare himself the führer of Germany and claim absolute power.

# A TURNING POINT

On June 30, 1934, an event known as Nacht der langen Messer, or the Night of the Long Knives, shocked Dodd. On this night and during the next few days, Hitler authorized the killing of hundreds of people who opposed him and his government.

[ These killings swept away any illusions that Dodd had for a reasonable and peaceful solution in Germany. ]

He recognized Hitler's ruthlessness and resolved not to seek another meeting with him unless forced to by official business.

In 1934, Dodd wrote in his diary that he did not see how peace and better relations could be achieved in Germany as long as men such as Hitler and his two top lieutenants, Hermann Göring and Joseph Goebbels, led the country. Dodd hoped that the German people would rise in outrage over the murders that had taken place in late June 1934. To his shock, they did not.

Many people in Germany and around the world believed Hitler's explanation—that the killings were necessary to suppress a rebellion that would have caused bloodshed across Germany. In truth, it was one of the first clues as to how far Hitler would go to maintain his grip on power.

Dodd warned officials back in the United States that Germany was preparing for war. Dodd urged America to abandon its isolationist policies and take action. Few people took Dodd's warnings seriously, though, and the United States remained on the sidelines.

In a 1936 letter to U.S. Secretary of State Cordell Hull, Dodd expressed his frustration at watching the German army increase in size and efficiency. No democratic country appeared willing to do anything to stop them. Dodd resolved to resign. By the end of December 1937, he and his family left Germany for home.

At a dinner given in his honor in January 1938 in New York City, Dodd declared, "Mankind is in grave danger, but democratic governments seem not to know what to do. If they do nothing, Western civilization, religious, personal, and economic freedom are in grave danger."

Dodd's words would prove to be prophetic. In March 1938, German troops marched into Austria to seize the nation by force and annex it to Germany. A few months later, in November 1938, anti-Semitism erupted in Kristallnacht, also known as the Night of Broken Glass. During two nights, Nazi Party officials and members of the SA and the Hitler Youth carried out violent riots against the Jews. Hundreds of synagogues and Jewish-owned homes and businesses were destroyed, and almost 100 Jewish citizens were killed. World War II and the Holocaust were at hand.

In this book, you will explore the roots of the Holocaust. You'll follow the unfolding of events that led to the Nazi Party carrying out its Final Solution—the mass extermination of Jewish people through industrialized death camps. Through it all, you will also hear stories of resilience and kindness in the darkest of times.

> By learning about the Holocaust, people around the world might stand up against discrimination and persecution, so that genocide on this scale may never happen again.

**The Nazis did not act alone in their mission to destroy the Jews and erase Jewish culture. People from other European countries that were occupied by the German army supported and assisted the Germans. Others stood by and did little while the Nazis carried out mass murder.**

## KEY QUESTIONS

- Why was William E. Dodd reluctant to believe that Hitler and the Nazi Party were dangerous?
- What do you already know about the Holocaust?
- Do you think the Holocaust could happen again in today's world?

## VOCAB LAB

Write down what you think each of the following words means. What root words can you find for help?

**diplomat, democracy, humane, isolationist, systematic, persecution, Nazi, genocide,** and **anti-Semitism**.

Compare your definitions with those of your friends or classmates. Did you all come up with the same meanings? Turn to the text and glossary if you need help.

# USE ART TO SHOW LIFE AND DEATH DURING THE HOLOCAUST

During the Holocaust, people created art while living in ghettos and concentration camps, or while in hiding. These pieces of art documented life in these places and showed events from the artists' perspectives. Created by professional artists and everyday people, these works of art provide a lasting snapshot of life and death during Hitler's rise to power.

* **You can examine some art created during the**

   inmate art Birkenau and Auschwitz concentration camps

   Holocaust ghetto artists

   Fernand Horn Van Horen

   a Holocaust art exhibit Illinois

  **Holocaust at these websites.**

* **After studying these paintings and drawings, what did you learn about life in the concentration camps and the experiences of the artists?**

  * How did the artist use their art to express emotions?

  * How did they use color (or lack of color) in the art?

  * What themes or symbols did you notice?

- **Even though you did not personally live through the Holocaust, you can still connect emotionally to the subject.** Using what you have learned about the Holocaust and the experience of those in the Jewish ghettos and concentration camps, create a piece of art to document life and death during this time. When creating your art, consider the following:

  - What form of art will you create?

  - Will your art be literal and illustrative or more abstract and impressionist?

  - What themes will you use in your art? Some examples include hope, fear, longing, despair, loss of childhood, and life before the Holocaust.

  - Will you use symbols in your art? What will they represent?

To investigate more, consider the artist Charlotte Salomon, a Jewish artist from Berlin, Germany. She painted a collection of autobiographical works known as *Life? Or Theatre?* Between 1940 and 1942, she created 1,325 watercolors. About 800 of these paintings were included in *Life? Or Theatre?* Salomon was murdered at Auschwitz in 1943. More people died at Auschwitz than at any other concentration camp. You can learn more about Salomon's life and explore how she used art to document life during the Holocaust at this website.

 Charlotte Salomon

### WHAT IS GENOCIDE?

Before 1944, the word *genocide* did not exist. In 1944, a Jewish lawyer from Poland named Raphael Lemkin wanted a way to describe the Nazi policies of systematic murder. He combined *geno* from the Greek word meaning "race" or "tribe" with *cide*, from a Latin word meaning "killing." Today, the word *genocide* refers to violent crimes committed against a group with the intention to destroy the group and its existence.

# Chapter 1 ▶
# The Jewish People and Anti-Semitism

What were the roots
of anti-Semitism?

SO ANTI-SEMITISM STARTED ABOUT 2,000 YEARS AGO?

WELL, NOT EXACTLY...

THAT'S WHEN THE ANCIENT ROMANS EXILED THE JEWISH PEOPLE FROM PALESTINE.

SINCE THEN THEY'VE BEEN A RELIGIOUS MINORITY WHEREVER THEY LIVED.

BECAUSE THEY WERE SEEN AS OUTSIDERS, THEY WERE OFTEN TREATED AS SCAPEGOATS.

IN SOME PLACES THEY WERE EVEN BLAMED FOR THE BLACK PLAGUE!

**The Jewish people have experienced discrimination for millennia in many different parts of the world.**

Founded more than 3,500 years ago, Judaism is one of the world's oldest religions. It developed in the Middle East, in an area that includes most of modern Israel, Jordan, and Syria. Almost 2,000 years ago, the ancient Romans defeated the Jewish people and occupied the land where they lived. The Romans exiled the Jews, driving them out of their homes.

Many Jewish people fled to other communities throughout Europe. They made new homes in every European country, from Portugal to Russia. Judaism developed differently in different areas, based on the influence of the local people and cultures.

Spain, Germany, and France were home to some of the largest Jewish settlements. In many of these communities, the Jewish people lived reasonably well. They were often protected by local rulers who valued their trading contacts in other countries.

# BEGINNINGS OF ANTI-SEMITISM

As Christianity spread throughout Europe, the Jewish people faced increasing discrimination and persecution because of their religion. One of the core beliefs of Christianity is that Jesus Christ, a Jewish preacher and healer believed to have lived in the Middle East 2,000 years ago, was the Messiah and the son of God. This belief caused a division between Christians and Jews, who do not believe that Jesus was the son of God.

According to the Christian gospels, which are part of Christianity's sacred texts, Jesus was put to death by crucifixion for claiming to be the king of the Jews. This claim was a crime under Jewish law. Also according to Christian gospels, Jesus rose from the dead three days after his death and appeared to several of his followers before joining God in heaven. The story of Jesus's death and resurrection serves as a foundation of the Christian religion.

[ The animosity against the Jews developed because many Christians blamed the Jewish people for the killing of Jesus. ]

Leaders of the Christian church encouraged this thinking and taught its followers that the Jews were responsible for the death of Jesus. Church readings about Jesus's crucifixion stirred up distrust and hatred of Jews. Christian religious performances told stories from the Bible that presented the Jews as villains who were enemies of Jesus. Some religious folklore portrayed the Jews as evil.

## POGROMS

From the seventeenth century, organized massacres of Jews took place in Russia and Eastern Europe. These massacres were called pogroms. The word *pogrom* comes from the Russian word for "devastation," and it means violent riots that persecute an ethnic or religious group, especially the Jews. Pogroms were often organized in local communities, sometimes with the encouragement of government officials and police. Perpetrators raped and murdered Jewish people. They stole and vandalized their property. Between 1918 and 1920, pogroms in Belarus and Poland killed tens of thousands of Jews.

In the Middle Ages, European Christians set out on a series of military campaigns called the Crusades. During the Crusades, the Christians fought Muslims for control of the Holy Land and Jerusalem, where Jesus was said to have lived his life and been crucified. While the soldiers fought in the Crusades, many Christians at home in Europe also believed it was their duty to fight against those they believed were the enemies of Christianity. They turned their violence against the most visible non-Christian group, the Jewish people.

## OPPRESSED AND EXILED

Throughout Europe, various communities passed laws that oppressed the Jewish people. In many places, Jews were not allowed to own land. They were barred from joining Christian trade guilds, which limited their ability to work and support their families.

> In some parts of Europe, Jews had to wear special badges or hats to mark them as different.

Unable to work in the trades, some Jews became money lenders or tax collectors to earn a living. In the Middle Ages, which lasted from the fifth to the fifteenth century, the Church banned Christians from being money lenders. Because communities still needed to borrow and lend money, the Jewish people filled this role. In some areas, Jews became tax collectors for local rulers. However, serving in these jobs made the Jews unpopular in their communities. When it comes time for people to pay back their loans or pay their taxes, they often blame their money troubles on the person who is doing the collecting.

---

## LIFE IN THE SHTETL

For centuries, Jews lived in small towns and market villages across Russia and Eastern Europe known as shtetls. In a shtetl, life was often hard, but there was also a strong sense of community and religion. The center of a shtetl was its shul, or synagogue. People prayed, studied, and gathered for social events such as weddings at the synagogue.

In the twentieth century, many Jews chose to leave the shtetl and move west. They migrated to the cities of Europe and the United States in search of more cultural and economic opportunities. There, they formed large urban communities, which replaced the shtetl as a center of Jewish life.

During this time, the Jewish people often moved from one land to another. Sometimes, they moved to escape outbreaks of violence. Other times, they were forced from their communities. Christian merchants often felt threatened by competition from Jewish merchants. They demanded that local rulers force the Jews to leave. Other times, communities expelled Jewish residents because of false accusations that Jews kidnapped and killed Christian children and used their blood in religious rituals. Can you think of a modern time when false news affected a group of people?

In 1290, King Edward I expelled the Jews from all of England. Expulsions also occurred in France, Portugal, Germany, Austria, and other European countries. In Spain, the Jewish people had lived in relative peace under the region's Islamic rule. When new Christian rulers took over the country, they wanted everyone in Spain to be Catholic. In 1492, they demanded that hundreds of thousands of Jews either convert to Christianity or leave the country. Many Jews created new homes in Eastern Europe, particularly in Poland and Russia.

## THE AGE OF ENLIGHTENMENT

In the 1700s, daily life for many Jews across Europe improved as a movement called the Enlightenment swept across the continent. The Enlightenment was a period of scientific and technological developments that challenged previously held views and beliefs. Voyages across the ocean revealed new people and cultures. Along with new ideas, the Enlightenment brought increased tolerance toward others. In this atmosphere, many Jews enjoyed more rights and freedoms.

### THE FRAMING OF CAPTAIN ALFRED DREYFUS

In 1894, Captain Alfred Dreyfus, a Jewish officer in the French army, was arrested for spying. He was put on trial for treason. During the trial, a mob of French citizens called him a traitor and chanted, "Death to the Jews," outside the courtroom. Although there was little evidence against him, the French court found Dreyfus guilty. Eventually, evidence emerged that proved Dreyfus was innocent and had been framed. He was pardoned, but the events surrounding this trial showed the existence of anti-Semitism in France.

In 1881, revolutionaries in Russia assassinated Czar Alexander II. The Jews were blamed for his death, which set off a period of violence and persecution. To escape, millions of Jews migrated to the Americas. In the United States, the number of Jewish people increased from about 50,000 in 1881 to more than 3.4 million in 1919.

In 1879, Wilhelm Marr, a German journalist, first used the word *anti-Semite* to describe people who hate the Jews. He blamed the Jews for everything that was wrong in Europe. Today, the word *anti-Semitism* means hatred or prejudice against Jewish people.

In 1789, the French Revolution overthrew the king and created the first republic in Europe. After the revolution, the French Jews were given legal equality with other French citizens. Other countries followed France's lead and granted Jewish people the rights of full citizens.

By the nineteenth century, many laws that had excluded the Jews from European life were lifted. Many Jews became involved in their communities, often serving as leaders in arts, science, business, and politics. In addition, feelings of nationalism increased in Europe. Almost everyone, including Jewish people, joined together in feeling patriotic about the country in which they lived.

However, despite these movements toward inclusion and nationalism, some people still saw the Jews as outsiders. They resented Jews who became successful. Although they had gained equal rights under the law, many Jews still experienced prejudice in their daily lives.

## IMPACT OF THE GREAT WAR

In 1914, the assassination of Archduke Franz Ferdinand of Austria served as the spark that ignited the First World War. From 1914 to 1918, the Central Powers of Germany, Austria-Hungary, and Turkey fought against the Allies of France, Great Britain, Russia, Italy, Japan, and eventually the United States.

The war ended in 1918 with the defeat of Germany and the Central Powers. It caused more death and destruction than any other conflict in the world's history. By the war's end in November 1918, nearly 10 million soldiers had been killed and around 21 million had been wounded. About 7 million civilians died as well.

The war ended with the Treaty of Versailles, a peace treaty signed near Paris, France, in 1919. The victorious Allies wanted to make sure that Germany would never go to war again. The treaty forced Germany to reduce its armies and give up land. The treaty also required Germany to take responsibility for the damages caused by the war and to pay enormous amounts of money in reparations to the Allies, particularly France.

> These conditions, along with the heavy casualties that Germany suffered during the war, left the German people humiliated.

The Great War, also known as World War I, devastated Germany. Two million young men were killed and 4.2 million were wounded. At home, civilians faced serious food shortages because of Allied blockades. Without being able to trade with other nations during the war, the economy fell apart. After the war, inflation in Europe and the burden of reparation payments further weakened the German economy.

## THE BLACK DEATH

From 1348 to 1354, a plague called the Black Death spread through Europe, killing one-third of the population. Confusion and fear of death led to a panic. People searched for someone to blame for the devastating sickness and mounting deaths. Prejudice against the Jewish community made them an easy target. Incorrectly blaming the Jewish people for bringing the Black Death upon them, some communities attacked and expelled Jews. In reality, the plague was spread by rats.

English soldiers in 1917

photo credit: Ernest Brooks

**KEY QUESTIONS**

- Have you ever heard the saying, "History repeats itself?" Do you think this is true? Why or why not?

- Why do religions change as the members of a religious group move around the world?

- Have you ever encountered or witnessed anti-Semitism? What were the circumstances?

In 1914, Germany had been Europe's greatest economy and military power. Now, the German military was defeated and its economy was in ruins. By 1921, the struggling country could not make the reparation payments that were required under the Treaty of Versailles. In response, French and Belgian troops invaded a section of Germany called the Ruhr Valley to seize coal and other factory products to make up for unpaid reparations. The result was more violence.

For the average German citizen, the post-war economy led to hardships at home. In order to help pay for expensive goods, the German government printed more money. With more money available, but goods still hard to find, the prices of everything skyrocketed. By 1923, inflation soared and people's savings were wiped out.

> Some Germans even burned money for heat because it was cheaper than buying fuel.

Conditions worsened during the Great Depression, which arrived in 1929. Many middle class Germans lost their jobs. By 1932, more than 6 million Germans were unemployed. People were desperate for money to pay for food, clothing, and housing. Some, who were unable to pay rent, were forced into the streets and became homeless. Those who were lucky enough to have jobs often worked for low wages in poor conditions. The future appeared bleak to the German people.

In the next chapter, we'll discover how this national catastrophe contributed to the rise of one of the most famous tyrants in the world—Adolf Hitler.

# MIGRATION OF THE JEWISH PEOPLE

After the defeat and exile of the Jewish people by the ancient Romans, the Jews spread to different countries. They brought Judaism to many corners of the world in the diaspora, or dispersion. Expulsions from European communities in the Middle Ages also forced the Jews to move to new lands.

- **Research the movements of the Jewish people from the Middle East into Europe.** Where did they go? What communities did they establish? Were they able to stay in these communities or were they exiled again? Where did they go?

- **Create a map that shows what you have learned about the movements of the Jewish people.** Consider these questions.

  - In what ways would a Jewish settlement in one location be different or similar to a Jewish settlement in another location?

  - How did the movement of the Jewish people affect Jewish culture?

  - How did the spread of the Jewish people contribute to anti-Semitism?

**VOCAB LAB**

Write down what you think each of the following words means. What root words can you find for help?

**nationalism, exile, inflation, intolerance, tolerance, oppress,** and **reparation**.

Compare your definitions with those of your friends or classmates. Did you all come up with the same meanings? Turn to the text and glossary if you need help.

To investigate more, imagine that you and your family are moving from your home to a new country. Choose a place on the map. Write a diary entry describing your travel to your new home. What people do you meet? What languages do they speak? What do you see on your trip? What new foods and experiences might you have? How do you feel about leaving home and moving to an unfamiliar place?

# Chapter 2 ▶
# The Rise of the Nazi Party

How did the events following World War I contribute to Hitler's rise in power?

Germany felt a lack of leadership after World War I and the population suffered economically, making people eager to listen to someone who offered immediate solutions.

After defeat in World War I, Germany fell into disarray. Germany's king, Kaiser Wilhelm II, abdicated his throne and fled to Holland. The German economy was in shambles, with unemployment and inflation soaring. Under the Versailles peace treaty, the great German army, a source of pride for the German people, was dismantled. The morale of the German people sank to an all-time low.

Humiliated by defeat, the German people resented the conditions forced on them by the Treaty of Versailles. The loss of land and the payment of enormous reparations made many wonder how their country could have fallen so low. They looked for a scapegoat, someone to blame for everything they had lost. They found that scapegoat in the Jewish people.

Blaming the Jews for Germany's losses allowed many German citizens to feel better about World War I. It helped them avoid taking responsibility for their part in the defeat. It also created an environment in which the Nazi Party could rise to power.

# THE WEIMAR REPUBLIC

After the kaiser abdicated, German leaders created a new democratic system of government called the Weimar Republic. They decided no monarch would rule the country. Instead, Germany would be a parliamentary democracy with a president, a parliament called the Reichstag, and a chancellor.

The German people elected the president as their head of state by popular vote. He controlled the military and could call for new Reichstag elections. In certain situations, the president could assume emergency powers that allowed him to suspend civil rights and operate without the consent of the Reichstag. Members of the Reichstag were also elected by a popular vote, with seats given to each political party in proportion to their share of the vote. Chosen from the majority party in the Reichstag, the chancellor appointed a cabinet of advisors and ran the day-to-day operations of the German government.

From the beginning, instability plagued the Weimar Republic. One of its first acts was signing the unpopular Treaty of Versailles. Although members of the Weimar Republic had little choice in the matter, signing the treaty made many German citizens distrust the new government. In addition, political parties in Germany constantly struggled for control, with assassinations and coups occurring regularly. Between 1919 and 1923, the cabinet changed nine times. No strong leader controlled the country.

While some people supported a democratic government, others believed that strong, military leadership was the only way to keep Germany safe and put an end to the instability and chaos. Still others believed that communism was the fairest way to run the country.

## HITLER SPEAKS IN 1933

Adolf Hitler was a charismatic speaker who persuaded millions of Germans to follow his party and his cause. In this video, you can watch one of his speeches from 1933. Why do you think people were drawn to him? What was it about his public speaking that made people feel he was a leader?

🔍 historical speech Adolf Hitler

Differences in political beliefs led to conflicts throughout Germany. Political parties often turned to violence to promote their ideas and assassinated those who opposed them. Extremist groups made several attempts to take over Germany. Why do you think political instability led to violence? Does this happen now?

## NATIONAL SOCIALIST GERMAN WORKERS' PARTY

One of the many political groups that rose up after World War I was the National Socialist German Workers' Party, also known as the Nazi Party. Founded in 1919, the Nazi Party promoted German pride and anti-Semitism. Party members, many of whom had military backgrounds, believed that the Treaty of Versailles was unjust. It burdened Germany with payments that were impossible to make.

> Soon after its founding, the Nazi Party welcomed a new member, a German army veteran named Adolf Hitler.

At the time, the Nazi Party had only about 40 members. Hitler knew that the German people were devastated by the war. A skilled public speaker, he gave impassioned speeches in the beer cellars of Munich, blaming outsiders for Germany's problems.

He denounced the Treaty of Versailles and proposed limiting German citizenship to people with German blood. His persuasive message united Germans and gave them a common enemy for their anger. By November 1921, the Nazi Party had grown to approximately 3,000 members.

Hitler quickly became the party's leader. Because many members had military backgrounds, the Nazi Party began to operate like a military organization. One section of the party, the Strumabteilung (SA) acted as Hitler's private army of stormtroopers. The Schutzstaffel, or SS, was another paramilitary arm of the Nazis. After the Night of the Long Knives in 1934, when Hitler ordered the SS to kill leaders of the SA, the SS grew in number and eventually became the leading paramilitary force in Nazi Germany. Later, the Gestapo, or the secret police of Nazi Germany, was a group under the control of the SS.

Hitler and Nazi Party members announced they'd be taking over the government in November 1923, but they didn't get far before they were arrested in Munich. Found guilty of treason, Hitler was sentenced to five years in prison. He served only nine months.

## INCREASING POPULARITY

After his unsuccessful attempt to overthrow the government, Hitler realized he would have to use democratic methods to take control of the country. In the 1924 Reichstag elections, the Nazi Party won only 3 percent of the vote, compared to the Social Democratic Party's 26 percent.

After the election, Hitler and the Nazi Party began a long-term campaign to bring Germans to their side. They held large political rallies, with banners and marching bands. Radio stations broadcasting the rallies reached thousands of Germans. They advertised in newspapers, leaflets, and posters to encourage people to support the Nazi Party.

[ By 1928, the Nazis had more than 100,000 members. ]

### MEIN KAMPF

While in prison, Hitler wrote a book titled *Mein Kampf* (*My Struggle*). This book outlined his political and anti-Semitic ideas. After World War I, Hitler was convinced that some people in Germany—specifically the Jews—had worked for Germany's defeat. Hitler argued that Germans were part of the Aryan race, one that was superior to all others. According to Hitler, the Aryans were destined to rule the world. He believed that the Jews were a separate, inferior race that continued to conspire against the German Aryans. To protect himself and the other Aryans, Hitler aimed to destroy both the Jews and communists. *Mein Kampf* is still available to read on the Internet and from bookstores. This is a work of propaganda and shouldn't be read as truth. Why is it important to remember this?

To gain support, the Nazis used the powerful appeal of uniforms, symbols, rallies, and salutes to energize and unify the German people. Designed after the salute of Italian fascists and ancient Romans and Greeks, the Nazi salute was used to show loyalty to Hitler. In the salute, a person's uplifted arm resembled a raised spear. Nazi supporters saluted and greeted each other and proclaimed, "Sieg Heil!" which meant "Victory and hail!" The Nazi flag was designed by Hitler and incorporated red, black, and white, the historical colors of Germany's flag. Red represented the social idea of Nazism, white represented nationalism, while the black swastika represented the Aryan struggle, or the belief that German blood had to be kept pure.

In 1929, the New York Stock Exchange collapsed and triggered a global economic crisis called the Great Depression. Millions of people lost their jobs and struggled to feed and clothe their families. In Germany, the people wanted strong leadership to take care of the crisis and end the suffering. Because the moderate government appeared unable to solve the country's problems, desperate people turned to political parties with more extreme ideas.

> For many Germans, the Nazi Party seemed to be the strongest party and the one best able to deal with Germany's problems.

The Nazis capitalized on the discontent of the middle class. Hitler promised to overturn the Treaty of Versailles and halt the reparation payments. He also promised to rebuild the German army, navy, and air force, which would decrease unemployment. Hitler promised to bring stability to the economy and defend against communism. This appealed to German business owners.

By the July 1932 Reichstag elections, support for the Nazi Party was higher than ever before. They won about 37 percent of the vote and became the largest single party in the German parliament. As its leader, Hitler demanded to be named chancellor.

At first, Germany's President Paul von Hindenburg resisted appointing him, as he did not trust Hitler's motives and feared giving him more power. In January 1933, Hindenburg finally relented and made Hitler Germany's chancellor. Hindenburg believed that he would be able to keep Hitler under control.

# SPREADING PROPAGANDA

The Nazis used extensive propaganda to spread their ideas. Joseph Goebbels served as Hitler's minister of propaganda. Playing upon the German people's fear of uncertainty, Goebbels designed campaigns and propaganda that portrayed Hitler as a strong man who could solve Germany's problems. Many posters even showed Hitler alongside a powerful spiritual light in the sky and a dove flying overhead, which was similar to depictions of Jesus.

Nazi propaganda was often anti-Semitic and spread the Nazis' theories of race. The Nazis claimed that Germans were descended from an Aryan race and were naturally superior to other races, particularly the Jews. These theories of race helped to make ordinary German citizens feel better about themselves and strengthened Nazi popular support, particularly with younger people. The Nazis distributed this propaganda in newspaper ads and leaflets. They continued to hold the large political rallies that had helped them gain support during the 1920s, and to broadcast these rallies on the radio.

## BEAR WITNESS ✡

In 1938, Adolf Hitler was named *Time* magazine's man of the year.

German soldiers gather at the Nazi Party rally grounds in Nuremberg.

photo credit: Kurt Wittig

# THE END OF DEMOCRACY

The Germans who voted for the Nazi Party in 1932 wanted a resurgence in Germany. They hoped for strong new leadership that could revive the economy for all. They did not outright support the extreme positions of the party. Instead, they expected that once the Nazis were in office, they would work with others and compromise. Hitler had other ideas.

Within 24 hours of taking office, Hitler called for new Reichstag elections to be held in March 1933. He believed that new elections would allow the Nazi Party to increase its hold on the German parliament. In the weeks leading up to the elections, the SA and SS launched a violent campaign against communists and other Nazi political enemies.

In late February 1933, the Reichstag burned down. The police arrested a young Dutch communist named Marinus van der Lubbe and imprisoned 4,000 other communists. Hitler used the Reichstag fire and the public's fear of communists to his advantage.

On February 28, the Nazis issued the Decree for the Protection of People and State, which was signed by President Hindenburg. Under the guise of protecting Germany from the threat of communism, the decree granted the government emergency powers and suspended several personal freedoms. These included the freedom of expression, the right of assembly, and privacy of communication.

[ It was the first step in breaking down Germany's democracy. ]

In the days leading up to the March elections, the Nazis unleashed an anti-communist and anti-Semitic campaign. They spread their propaganda on the radio, in newspapers and leaflets, and at rallies. In the March elections, the Nazis increased their share of the Reichstag to nearly 44 percent, but failed to gain a majority. Hitler would need a new tactic to gain complete control.

After the March elections, Hitler proposed a new law to the Reichstag called the Enabling Act. The Enabling Act gave the German cabinet the power to enact laws without the Reichstag. Because Chancellor Hitler controlled the cabinet, the Enabling Law would effectively give Hitler and the Nazis control of Germany.

> The Reichstag passed the Enabling Act, giving Hitler and the Nazi Party the power to make laws without approval from the German parliament.

With the power of the Enabling Act, Hitler and the Nazis next moved to eliminate any remaining opposition to their leadership and agenda. In April 1933, they established a concentration camp in the town of Dachau, which was located near Munich. The camp was designed to hold political prisoners. In May, the Nazis took over Germany's trade unions and merged them into the state-controlled German Labour Front (DAF). They arrested union leaders and sent them to Dachau.

During the next few months, the SA and SS raided the offices of opposing political parties. They destroyed property, seized assets, and arrested opposing leaders. By the end of June, most political parties agreed to cease operations. By July, a law stated that the Nazi Party was the only legal party in Germany.

**Using the new emergency powers of the government under the Decree for the Protection of People and State, the SS and SA arrested thousands of communists and Nazi opponents. Once arrested, the prisoners could be held indefinitely without a trial.**

## BEAR WITNESS ✡

Some people suspect that the Nazis burned down the Reichstag building themselves.

# EXPANDING NAZI CONTROL

## THE ENABLING ACT

Passed in 1933, the Enabling Act allowed the German cabinet to introduce legislation without going through the Reichstag. You can read the act at this website.

GHDI Enabling Act

The Nazis worked to expand their influence by controlling people's actions and thoughts. Propaganda Minister Joseph Goebbels instructed the press and other writers, along with scientists, to express only Nazi ideas. Books written by Jewish authors and others considered to be opponents of the Nazis were removed from public libraries. In 1933, Nazis publicly burned these books in Berlin and other towns. Artists and scientists who refused to comply with Nazi demands were forced into silence or to leave the country.

The Nazis also took over the education of Germany's youngest citizens. Teachers who did not agree with Nazi policies were removed. The Nazis introduced new textbooks in schools that reflected the party's views and values.

In August 1934, President Hindenburg died. After his death, Hitler combined the roles of president and chancellor. He took the title of führer and assumed sole control of the country.

A public book burning in 1933

photo credit: National Archives

# NAZI TREATMENT OF JEWS

Anti-Semitism and the persecution of Jews was a main part of Nazi ideology. In the Nazi Party's 1920 party program, the Nazis pledged to segregate Jews from German society and to take away their political, legal, and civil rights. Soon after Hitler and the Nazis took control in Germany, they began to implement their promise to persecute German Jews. Between 1933 and 1939, they passed more than 400 decrees and regulations to restrict the Jews' public and private lives.

In the beginning, legislation focused on limiting the ability of Jews to participate in public life in Germany. On April 7, 1933, the Law for the Restoration of the Professional Civil Service excluded Jewish employees from state service. Also in 1933, other laws restricted the number of Jewish students at German schools and restricted the work of Jewish doctors and lawyers. The city of Berlin banned Jewish lawyers from working on legal matters, while Jewish doctors in Munich were forbidden to treat non-Jewish patients.

The licenses of Jewish tax consultants were revoked. And the Nazi government forbade Jewish actors to perform on stage or screen. Some local governments also passed regulations that limited the ability of Jews to slaughter animals according to religious practice, preventing them from following Jewish dietary laws.

When Hitler came to power in 1933, few people could anticipate the horrors that would happen during the next decade. Although some were alarmed by the anti-Semitism promoted by Hitler's Nazi Party, most believed the situation was temporary. They decided that things would get better. They decided to wait. What might have gone differently if they had acted?

## BEAR WITNESS ✡

The Nazis focused on influencing and recruiting young Germans through youth movement activities, including the Hitler Youth for boys and League of German Girls. Social pressures forced many young people to join these organizations, where they were expected to show blind obedience and loyalty to Hitler and the Nazi regime. Children wore uniforms and participated in fitness and endurance activities. Why was physical strength seen as a desirable trait in Nazi recruits?

# THE NUREMBERG LAWS

In September 1935, the Nazi Party held a rally in Nuremberg. At the rally, leaders announced new laws that worsened conditions for the Jews. Known as the Nuremberg Laws, these laws were based on the Nazis' theories of race and their belief in a superior Aryan race that must be kept pure.

The Nuremberg Laws denied citizenship to German Jews. They made it illegal for Jews to marry or have sexual relations with a German or a person with German-related blood. These laws also deprived the Jews of many of their political rights—they were no longer able to vote or hold public office. The Nuremberg Laws identified anyone who had three or four Jewish grandparents as Jewish, regardless of the person's religion. Many Germans who did not practice Judaism or who had converted to Christianity years earlier found themselves labeled and persecuted as Jews.

> A rush of anti-Semitic legislation followed that effectively segregated the Jewish population.

The laws reinforced the idea that the Jews were outsiders in Germany. Jewish people could not be admitted to municipal hospitals. Jewish officers were kicked out of the army.

In 1937 and 1938, the Nazis also attempted to remove the Jews from the Germany economy. They passed laws and regulations to prevent them from earning a living.

They required the Jews to register all property and assets, both in Germany and in foreign countries. The Nazis also began to "Aryanize" all businesses by firing Jewish workers and managers and transferring Jewish-owned companies to non-Jewish Germans at bargain prices. Between 1933 and 1938, these policies reduced the number of Jewish-owned businesses by about two-thirds.

# KRISTALLNACHT

On November 9 and 10, 1938, a wave of violence spread throughout Germany and German-occupied lands. It was called Kristallnacht, or the Night of Broken Glass, for the shattered glass that lined German streets after the violent pogrom.

The violence erupted after the assassination of Ernst vom Rath, a German embassy official in Paris. A 17-year-old Polish Jew shot vom Rath on November 7, after his parents, Jews with Polish citizenship, were expelled from their longtime home in Germany.

[
The Nazis used the assassination as an excuse to launch a night of anti-Semitic violence.
]

The violence erupted late in the night of November 9 and continued into the early morning. Members of the SA and Hitler Youth attacked Jewish homes, businesses, and synagogues.

## PROTECTING INDIVIDUAL RIGHTS

In the United States, the Bill of Rights protects the basic individual rights of every citizen, including freedom of the press, freedom of religion, freedom of speech, and freedom of assembly. If you lived in Nazi Germany, these rights would have been suspended by Hitler's government. Without these rights, life would be very different. Without freedom of speech, you could be arrested for speaking out against the government. News outlets would only report stories approved by the government. You might not be allowed to gather with your friends. Police could search your house at any time, without a warrant. How would you feel if these freedoms were taken away from you?

## CONCENTRATION CAMPS APPEAR

With Hitler and the Nazis in control, the local police, the SA, and the SS gathered up anyone who opposed them. Their prisoners included thousands of communists, socialists, church leaders, and others. At first, these prisoners were held in local prisons. As the number of prisoners grew, temporary buildings were constructed to hold them. This system proved inefficient, so the Nazis built camps specifically designed to hold large numbers of prisoners, called concentration camps. The first camp opened on April 1, 1933, at Dachau, near Munich. By 1945, the Nazis had built more than 20,000 concentration camps across the land they occupied, under the control of the SS. In later years, the Nazis used the concentration camps to hold millions of Jews and other persecuted people.

Many wore civilian clothes to support the false idea that the violence was public reaction instead of a coordinated attack on Jews. Yet party leaders gave specific instructions not to harm non-Jewish Germans or their property, or foreigners. During the pogrom, rioters destroyed 267 synagogues throughout German-controlled land. Approximately 7,500 Jewish-owned businesses were vandalized and looted.

In the cities of Berlin and Vienna, the pogroms became particularly violent. Mobs of SA men roamed the streets and attacked Jews in their homes. Police and the SS arrested as many as 30,000 Jewish men and sent most of them to concentration camps. At least 91 Jews died during Kristallnacht.

> It was the first time the Nazis imprisoned such a large number of people based solely on their heritage.

Immediately after Kristallnacht, German leaders blamed the Jews for the violence and destruction. They imposed a fine of 1 billion Reichsmark on the Jewish community. The government also confiscated all insurance payouts to Jewish people whose homes and businesses were damaged. Without insurance payments, the Jewish people were left to pay for all repairs themselves.

After Kristallnacht, the Nazi anti-Semitic policy became more radical. The Nazis expanded their efforts to remove Jews entirely from German society and economy. They banned Jews from all public schools and universities, cinemas, theaters, and sports facilities. In many communities, "Aryan" zones barred Jews from entering.

In addition, the government required all Jews to identify themselves. Beginning in January 1939, all Jewish people had to add "Israel" and "Sara" to their given names. All Jews were required to carry identification cards that indicated they were Jewish. In addition, Jewish passports were stamped with the letter "J." How did forcing Jewish people to identify themselves contribute to discrimination?

## EXPANDING THE THIRD REICH

Hitler was determined to increase Germany's land by any means necessary, even war. In 1938 and 1939, he was able to accomplish this without fighting. In March 1938, German troops occupied Austria, with the support of many Austrians who favored unifying the two countries. Although the occupation violated the Treaty of Versailles, no country protested Germany's actions.

In September 1938, Hitler had his sights on the Sudetenland, a northwestern section of Czechoslovakia that had 3 million German-speaking citizens. Hitler called for the unification of all Germans. Germany demanded that the German people in the Sudetenland be allowed to join Germany and threatened an invasion. In September, the leaders of Great Britain, France, and Italy met with Hitler at the Munich Conference to discuss the situation. Wanting to avoid a German invasion of Czechoslovakia and war, the leaders agreed to allow Germany to annex Sudetenland.

Six months after the Munich Conference, Hitler went back on the agreement. German forces invaded the rest of Czechoslovakia in March 1939. Soon after that, the world erupted into World War II. We'll learn about this global battle in the next chapter.

**BEAR WITNESS** ✡

The word *reich* means "realm" in German. Hitler's government was called the Third Reich or the Third Empire. The first reich is the Holy Roman Empire. The second reich is the German empire between 1871 and 1918.

**KEY QUESTIONS**

- Could a man like Hitler gain control in a democratic country today? Why or why not?
- Why were the Nazis able to take control of Germany without much resistance on the part of the populace?
- Why did Hitler blame the Jews for Germany's loss in World War I and the subsequent hardships?

## VOCAB LAB

Write down what you think each of the following words means. What root words can you find for help?

**scapegoat**, **Great Depression**, **parliamentary democracy**, **coup**, **fascists**, **swastika**, **propaganda**, **resurgence**, **Enabling Act**, **Aryan**, **concentration camp**, **ideology**, **Nuremberg Laws**, **Kristallnacht**.

Compare your definitions with those of your friends or classmates. Did you all come up with the same meanings? Turn to the text and glossary if you need help.

# CREATING PROPAGANDA

The Nazis used propaganda to spread their ideas and policies. Propaganda is defined as biased information intended to shape public opinion and behavior. After the Nazis gained power in 1933, Hitler created a Reich Ministry of Public Enlightenment and Propaganda and appointed Joseph Goebbels as its leader. The ministry's goal was to communicate the Nazi message through art, music, theater, films, books, radio, newspapers, and other educational materials.

- **Some propaganda was intended to remind German citizens of the struggle against foreign and Jewish enemies.** Propaganda also attempted to persuade the people to accept the measures to oppress the Jews.

- **You can examine some of the propaganda created during the Holocaust at the following websites.**

United States Holocaust Memorial Museum (site may require Flash, see resources for URL)

United States Holocaust Memorial Museum: Nazi Propaganda Photograph

Nazi Propaganda 1933–1945

BBC UK: Nazi Propaganda

- **After studying examples, what did you learn about how the Nazis used propaganda?**

  - Who was the intended audience?

  - How did the propaganda appeal to its audience? What made the propaganda effective?

  - What themes or symbols did you notice?

- **Using what you have learned about propaganda, create your own propaganda piece.** When creating it, consider the following.

  - What form will you use?

  - Who is your intended audience?

  - What message are you trying to convey or behavior are you trying to encourage?

  - Will you use symbols in your propaganda? What will they represent?

To investigate more, consider that, even today, people use propaganda to influence others and spread their ideas. What examples of propaganda can you find in your community? Have you witnessed propaganda about world events? How did it affect your perception? How can you tell that it is propaganda and how can you guard against propaganda?

### Inquire & Investigate

### REMEMBERING: ANTI-SEMITISM IN GERMANY

Born in 1924 in Karlsruhe, Germany, Hanne Hirsch Liebmann remembers being harassed for being Jewish in 1930s Germany. During the boycott of April 1933, her family's photography studio's windows were plastered with slurs, including, "Jew, Jew, don't go to the Jew!" You can hear her memories and testimony at this website.

🔍 Hanne Hirsch Liebmann USHMM

# CONSIDERING DIFFERENT VIEWPOINTS

In 1930s Germany, daily life could be very different for teens, depending on their backgrounds and beliefs.

- **Imagine that you are a Jewish teen living in Berlin.** What is your life like? How do you feel about the increasing power of Hitler and the Nazi Party? How has it affected your life?

- **Compare the experience of a Jewish teen to that of a Christian teen living in Berlin.** How would your life be different from your Jewish neighbor? How would it be the same?

- **Create a chart.** Use it to compare and contrast the lives and experiences of the Jewish and Christian teens. What kinds of aspects of teen life should go on your chart?

Hitler earned millions from sales of *Mein Kampf*. From 1933 to 1945, every newlywed German couple received a free copy of the book.

To investigate more, put yourself in the shoes of one of these teens. Write a diary entry from either the Jewish or Christian teen's point of view. Make sure to use description and sensory details in your entry.

# Chapter 3 ▶

# Persecution and World War II

Why did Hitler decide to begin invading other European countries?

The chaos and confusion of war made it possible for the Nazis to act on their racist theories and spread the German people farther into other lands.

||||||||||||||||||||||||||||||||||||||||||||||

On September 1, 1939, German armies invaded Poland. For Hitler, it was another step toward gaining lebensraum, or living space, in Eastern Europe for the German people. Yet he also saw war as a way to carry out the Nazi's racial policies across a wider European area.

According to Hitler's propaganda minister, Joseph Goebbels, war made it possible for the Nazis to solve a variety of problems that they could not solve during peacetime. In war, the German people united against common enemies, both real and perceived. Plus, under the excuse of war, the Third Reich was free to act without restraint against the Jews.

The Nazi invasion destroyed the Polish army within weeks. Poland's capital city, Warsaw, surrendered in a month. Honoring a treaty they had signed to come to Poland's defense, Great Britain and France declared war on Germany. World War II had begun.

# THE OCCUPATION OF EUROPE

After the invasion of Poland, Nazi armies continued their sweep through Europe. On April 9, 1940, Germany invaded Denmark and Norway, quickly conquering both. On May 10, the Germans entered Belgium, the Netherlands, and France. The Netherlands fell in five days, while Belgium fell within a few weeks.

The French army retreated in the face of German troops. On June 14, 1940, France's capital city of Paris fell to the Germans. On June 22, France signed an armistice with Germany. It agreed that the northern half of the country would be occupied by German forces while Italy, a German ally, occupied a small section in the southeast. The armistice also established a regime that collaborated with Germany in the French city of Vichy.

During the summer of 1940, the German air force, called the Luftwaffe, bombed Great Britain to weaken the British before a planned invasion. But the British Royal Air Force (RAF) put up a stiff fight. Between July and October 1940, the skies above Britain were filled with dueling pilots. Faced with stronger-than-anticipated British resistance, the Germans postponed their plans to invade Britain. Instead, they turned their attention to the eastern front.

Hitler wanted to expand the German Reich farther into the east. On April 6, 1941, Germany invaded Greece and Yugoslavia. The German armies met strong resistance from the Greeks and Yugoslavs, but both eventually fell to the Germans.

The Nazis then turned against their former ally, the Soviet Union. The area that is now known as Russia was called the Soviet Union from 1922 to 1991. During the winter of 1941, Nazi Germany planned a spring offensive against the Soviets. Because the invasion of Greece and Yugoslavia took longer than expected, the Nazis were forced to delay their Soviet offensive until late June.

By late spring 1941, the Soviet army was the only major land force in Europe left to stand against the Germans. And on June 22, 1941, the Germans invaded the Soviet Union in violation of the German-Soviet Pact of 1939.

[ Hitler and the German army looked unstoppable. ]

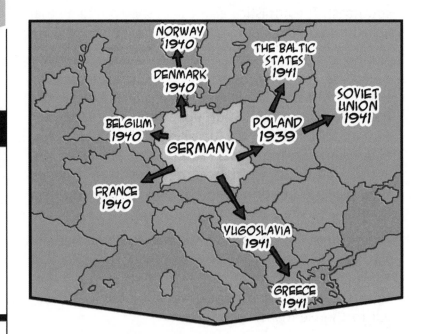

# PERSECUTION INTENSIFIES

As World War II erupted in Europe, the situation for Jewish people living in German-controlled territory grew even more dangerous. As the Germans took control of an area, they implemented their anti-Jewish policies there.

They defined and identified the Jews. Then, they barred the Jews from many jobs, including university and civil service jobs, teaching, and practicing as lawyers and doctors. The Nazis took over and "Aryanized" Jewish businesses. They also restricted and isolated Jews in society. They banned Jewish students from schools and public facilities. The Jews were forced to follow nighttime curfews and travel restrictions.

As Germany occupied more land in Europe, millions of Jews came under the control of the Nazis. In Poland alone, there were more than 2 million Jewish people. From the beginning, the German army treated foreign Jews with great cruelty. By September 1939, Reinhard Heydrich, the head of the Main Security Office of the SS, issued an order to force the Jews to live in separate areas within a city, called a ghetto. It was a short-term solution to contain and control the Jews. Later, the Nazi regime would act on a more permanent solution.

# LIVING IN THE GHETTO

Jewish people living across Poland and other occupied lands were moved to ghettos set up in cities. In Poland, the first ghetto was established in Piotrków Trybunalski on October 28, 1939. Other ghettos opened soon after in cities such as Lodz, Warsaw, Lublin, Krakow, Bialystok, Lvov, and Vilna.

## YELLOW STAR OF DAVID

On September 1, 1941, Reinhard Heydrich, chief of the Reich Main Security Office, ordered all Jews over the age of six in Germany and German-controlled lands to wear a yellow Star of David with the word "Jew" on their clothing. The star became a badge to publicly identify the Jewish people. It was not a new idea. Since medieval times, societies had forced Jewish citizens to wear identifying badges. The German authorities used the badge to publicly humiliate Jews and to mark them for discrimination. The star also allowed officials to easily identify Jews for deportation.

Between 1939 and 1945, the Nazis created hundreds of ghettos across Europe. They used these areas to confine, control, and restrict the Jews.

At first, some ghettos were open and Jews could travel in and out of them. Before long, the Nazis built walls or barbed wire fences around the ghettos. The Warsaw Ghetto was closed by 11 miles of walls, while the Lodz Ghetto was sealed with wooden fences and barbed wire. Jews were not allowed to leave the ghetto or have contact with anyone outside. These closed ghettos cut off Jewish residents from the general population.

Conditions in the ghettos were harsh and crowded. In Warsaw, the ghetto took up only 2.4 percent of the city's land, yet it held 30 percent of the city's people. Rooms and apartments built for four people often housed 10 to 15 people. Families lived in constant fear of being deported or conscripted into forced labor.

The people often had little to eat and many starved to death. With a lack of clean water and no sewage systems, diseases such as typhus quickly spread. Hundreds of thousands of people died from disease, starvation, and exposure.

The wall around the ghetto in Warsaw

Despite the awful conditions, the Jewish people attempted to live as normally as possible. Children learned at makeshift schools. Rabbis held religious services, even though it was against the law. And many people created works of music, poetry, and art while living in the ghettos.

# THE JUDENRAT

The Nazi SS set up and administered each ghetto. To run daily affairs, they appointed a Judenrat, or a Jewish council, of local Jewish officials to govern the community. The council was responsible for controlling the ghetto and carrying out Nazi orders. This included transferring Jews from other areas into the ghetto, maintaining order in the ghetto, and issuing food rations. The council was also made to provide Jewish workers to the Nazis for forced labor.

[ Members of the Judenrat often found themselves in extremely difficult situations. ]

Following Nazi orders increased the suffering of their friends and neighbors. Disobeying the orders, however, often led to retribution against the Jews and even more suffering. Many councils tried to improve the ghetto by establishing organizations such as orphanages, hospitals, and aid societies.

When the Nazis began to empty the ghettos, they demanded the council supply the names of those to be deported. If the council refused, the Nazis took a larger number of ghetto residents. How did this tactic help divide the Jews? Did it serve to unite them in any way?

## WORK IN THE LODZ GHETTO

In Lodz, factories and workshops used ghetto residents as forced labor to make goods for the German war effort. The chairman of the Lodz Judenrat, Mordechai Chaim Rumkowski, believed that if Lodz proved to be useful for the German war effort, he could save the lives of Lodz residents. He set up a system of workshops that employed thousands of Jews. Workers labored for long hours in exchange for small rations. Anyone who did not cooperate was punished. More than 100 factories produced all types of goods, including hats, uniforms, boots, rubber, carpets, and even sausage. Because of the productivity of the Lodz workers, some of the men and women of Lodz were able to survive after other ghettos in Poland had been emptied and their residents sent to the death camps.

# THE WARSAW GHETTO

Before World War II, Warsaw was the largest center of Jewish life in Europe. As the war began, it became the largest ghetto, with more than 400,000 residents. The Nazis established the Warsaw Ghetto on October 12, 1940. Entire neighborhoods were evacuated, with moving schedules posted on billboards.

Jews and non-Jewish Polish people were forced out of Polish neighborhoods. During the last two weeks of October 1940, approximately 138,000 Jews and 113,000 Christian Poles were relocated. They took only the belongings that they could load onto a wagon. Anything left behind was confiscated. Think about the things in your home that you'd be unable to lift onto a wagon, the things you'd have to leave behind. What would you miss?

Tens of thousands of Warsaw Ghetto residents worked in forced labor for the Germans. They worked long hours for low pay and often endured brutal treatment at the hands of their supervisors.

On November 16, 1940, the Nazis walled in the Warsaw Ghetto. Conditions deteriorated quickly and food became even scarcer. The Germans allocated food supplies for people in Warsaw according to a priority schedule. The Jews of the Warsaw Ghetto were at the bottom of the list. During 1941, 43,000 ghetto residents died inside the ghetto from starvation and disease.

To survive, many ghetto residents turned to smuggling. At first, smugglers simply moved goods in and out of the ghetto past inattentive guards. Out of desperation, they developed more creative methods to move goods.

Connected houses that straddled the ghetto border became transfer points. Holes in walls and barbed wire fences could be covered up during the day and removed at night to quickly move goods. Carts that carried the dead to be buried outside the ghetto came back with smuggled goods. Even children learned how to slip goods into the ghetto.

In the eyes of the Nazis, the ghettos were only a temporary solution to what they called the "Jewish question." At first, the Nazis planned to deport the Jews from German land. But when this plan did not work, they came up with another idea to rid Europe of Jews. In the summer of 1942, the Germans began to gather the residents of the ghettos. They loaded them onto trains for their next destination—the Nazi concentration camps. By late summer 1944, there were no ghettos left in Eastern Europe.

Jewish workers in the Warsaw Ghetto

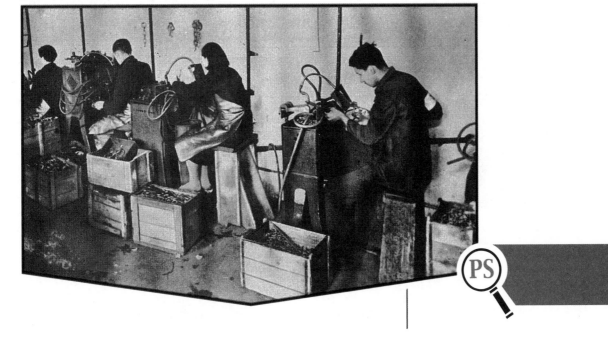

# THE NAZI EUTHANASIA PROGRAM

Mass murder by the Nazis began slowly, years before millions of Jews were exterminated in death camps. In October 1939, Hitler directed his personal physician, Dr. Karl Brandt, and Chancellery chief Philipp Bouhler to authorize Nazi doctors to put to death those people considered unsuited to live. With this order, the Nazi euthanasia program began. Men, women, and children who were physically or mentally disabled or emotionally disturbed were systematically murdered.

Under this program, all psychiatric institutions, hospitals, and homes for the chronically ill in Germany were ordered to send in a survey of patients. Nazi medical experts reviewed the forms and decided which patients should live or die. The patients determined to be unsuited to live were transported to six main killing sites.

At first, the patients were killed by starvation. Later, the Nazis used lethal doses of sedatives to kill the handicapped. Eventually, gassing replaced other killing methods. In a gas chamber disguised as a shower, a lethal gas was released that could kill up to 20 people at a time. Afterward, camp workers burned the bodies in a crematorium.

Families of the patients killed were told that their loved ones were being transferred in order to receive better care and treatment. They were not allowed to visit. Later, they received a condolence letter and a physician-signed death certificate that notified them of their relative's death.

Many in the German medical community rationalized the killings by arguing that these people were considered unworthy of life and they took away resources from healthy German people. Money spent on their care could be better used to support German workers and families. Hitler understood that during war, it was easy to forget the value of human life. He said that wartime was the best time to eliminate the incurably ill from the Germany population.

The Roman Catholic Church protested the so-called mercy killings. They openly challenged the Nazis, saying that it was the duty of Christians to oppose the taking of human life even at the expense of their own lives.

Eventually, the opposition of the church appeared to halt the euthanasia program. On August 24, 1941, nearly two years after it started, the euthanasia program appeared to end. In fact, it continued in secret. An estimated 200,000 to 250,000 people were killed in the Nazi euthanasia program.

The euthanasia program was just the beginning of the mass murder perpetrated by the Nazi regime. The euthanasia program was a preview of how the Nazis would eventually try to rid Europe of its Jewish population. You'll learn about this method, called the Final Solution, in the next chapter.

**The vast majority of people living in the ghettos died from disease or starvation, were shot, or were deported to killing centers.**

## VOCAB LAB

Write down what you think each of the following words means. What root words can you find for help?

**armistice**, **collaborate**, **Luftwaffe**, **domination**, **rationalize**, **ghetto**, **deport**, **conscript**, **retribution**, **Judenrat**, **smuggling**, **euthanasia**, and **crematorium**.

Compare your definitions with those of your friends or classmates. Did you all come up with the same meanings? Turn to the text and glossary if you need help.

### KEY QUESTIONS

- **Why was it easier to carry out extreme mistreatment of a vast number of people in wartime than in peacetime?**

- **Why do you think the other countries of the world didn't do more to stop Nazi Germany from taking control of other European countries?**

# DOCUMENT LIFE IN THE GHETTO

During the Holocaust, many Jews wrote about their lives and experiences in letters and diaries while living in ghettos and concentration camps. Some letters expressed the writer's hope and determination to survive. Others documented the details of everyday life. Because so many people did not survive, these documents are important sources of information of what life was like for Jews under Nazi rule.

---

- **You can read examples of letters and diary entries that describe life in the ghettos here.**

Diary of a Jewish youth named Yarden living in Lodz

Eva Heyman on the ghettoization of the Jews in Hungary

Hersh Wasser on hardship in the Warsaw Ghetto

From Ringelblum's Diary: As the Ghetto is Sealed Off, Jews and Poles Remain in Contact

- **You can also examine a photograph of Jews moving into the Kovno Ghetto in Lithuania.**

Holocaust encyclopedia move into Kovno Ghetto photo

- **Imagine that you are a Jewish teen living in one of the Nazi ghettos.** Document your life and experiences in a letter or diary entry.

  - Where do you live?

  - What conditions and hardships do you face?

  - How do you survive?

  - Who is there with you?

  - In what ways is your life the same as it was before living the ghetto? How has it changed?

To investigate more, imagine that you and your family have just been given a few hours to prepare to move into a ghetto. Jews were allowed to bring only the personal belongings that they could carry or load onto one small wagon. What would you bring with you from your former life and home? What would you leave behind? Explain your choices. How would they differ from the choices of members of your family?

# Chapter 4

# The Final Solution: Extermination

What problem was the Final Solution supposed to solve?

WHY WAS IT CALLED "THE FINAL SOLLUTION"?

THE NAZIS SAW THE EXISTENCE OF JEWISH PEOPLE AS A PROBLEM.

SO FIRST THEY TRIED TO GET THE JEWS TO LEAVE THEIR COUNTRY.

THEN THEY MADE THEM LIVE IN GHETTOS AND CONCENTRATION CAMPS.

THEN FINALLY THEY TRIED TO KILL ALL OF THEM, WHICH WAS...

"THE FINAL SOLUTION."

NOW I GET IT, BUT I REALLY WISH I DIDN'T.

**The Nazis believed that the Aryan race had to be protected from undesirable blood, so they devised a plan to kill anyone who was not physically and culturally Aryan.**

On June 22, 1941, the German army invaded the Soviet Union. The Soviets were quickly overwhelmed by the 3 million German soldiers. Within a month, the Germans captured the Baltic states of Latvia, Lithuania, and Estonia. In September, the Ukrainian capital city of Kiev fell and Leningrad was under attack.

Hundreds of thousands of Soviet soldiers were captured or killed. By the first days of December, German troops reached Moscow and forced the Soviet government to flee.

Despite early gains in the Soviet Union, the German plan for a quick victory fell apart. Supply problems, the harsh Russian winter, and stronger-than-anticipated resistance from Soviet troops stalled the German advance near Leningrad. On December 6, the Soviets pushed the Germans back from Moscow. In the fighting, the Germans suffered a large number of casualties. In the spring of 1942, the Germans launched another offensive in the Soviet Union. However, the Germans again met fierce resistance from Soviet troops.

> The invasion of the Soviet Union marked a turning point in the Holocaust. Previously, the Germans had rounded up Jews in occupied territories and sent them to live in segregated ghettos. Now, they took much more extreme action.

# MOBILE KILLING SQUADS

The Nazis believed that Jews were inferior to Aryans. Nazis considered these people to be barely human. They felt that in order to ensure the supremacy of the Aryan race, it was essential to eliminate anyone who didn't fit into this category.

During the Soviet invasion, the Germans began killing Jews in a systematic way. Small units of SS and police called Einsatzgruppen, or Special Deployment Groups, traveled with German troops. In Poland, the Einsatzgruppen had rounded up the Jews and forced them into ghettos. In the Soviet Union, they were told to kill any Jew they found.

As the Germans advanced, the mobile killing squads acted quickly, taking the Jews by surprise. When an area was invaded, the Einsatzgruppen and other German army units rounded up Jews, Communist Party officials, and Romani, including women and children. The soldiers took them outside of town and shot them. They dug ditches and filled them with piles of bodies.

Local residents could hear the gunshots and the cries of the victims. Most did nothing to stop the murders—they were terrified. In some areas, such as in Lithuania and Latvia, the German army and SS encouraged local people to murder its Jewish citizens, taking advantage of local anti-Semitism.

## MOBILE KILLING SQUAD COMMANDER TESTIMONY

After the Holocaust, one of the Einsatzgruppen commanders described a typical mobile killing squad action.

*"The Einsatz unit would enter a village or town and order the prominent Jewish citizen to call together all Jews for the purpose of 'resettlement.' They were requested to hand over their valuables and shortly before execution to surrender their outer clothing. They were transported to the place of executions, usually an antitank ditch, in trucks—always only as many as could be executed immediately.
. . . Then they were shot, kneeling or standing . . . and the corpses thrown into the ditch."*

In September 1941, the Germans captured Kiev, the capital city of Ukraine. Soon after, the Germans ordered the killing of all of Kiev's Jews. They ordered the city's Jews to appear at the Jewish cemetery. From the cemetery, the Germans marched the Jews two miles to the Babi Yar ravine. They forced the Jews to strip naked. Then, they shot every single man, woman, and child in the ravine, piling body upon body. More than 33,000 Jews were killed at Babi Yar. In the following months, the Germans killed Romani and Soviet prisoners of war at the ravine.

In August 1943, as the Soviet Army advanced, the Germans dug up the mass graves at Babi Yar and burned the bodies in an attempt to destroy the evidence of mass murder.

The mobile killing units murdered approximately 1.2 million Jews, one at a time. About 25 percent of all Jews murdered in the Holocaust were shot by the SS mobile killing squads. The victims' bodies were piled high in mass graves throughout the Soviet territories.

The Einsatzgruppen men who carried out these murders were ordinary German citizens. They characterized their actions as special actions, executive measures, and appropriate treatment. Yet the personal nature of this type of killing affected many of the Einsatzgruppen.

> Nazi officials realized that they needed to find a more impersonal and efficient way to kill the Jews.

## THE WANNSEE CONFERENCE

In the beginning, the Nazis planned to rid Germany of the Jews by forcing them to move to other countries. But that plan proved unworkable when few countries allowed entry to Jewish immigrants. And as the Germans occupied more land in Europe, more Jews fell under their control. Between 1933 and 1938, about 155,000 Jews left Germany. When Germany annexed Austria, 200,000 Jews were added to the Third Reich. And when Germany occupied Poland, more than 2 million Polish Jews were added to German-controlled land. Forced emigration for this many people was not a realistic solution.

In January 1942, a Nazi official named Reinhard Heydrich called a meeting of several top government officials. They met at a villa in Wannsee, outside of Berlin. Heydrich introduced the agenda—the Final Solution to the Jewish question.

The men around the table understood that Heydrich's Final Solution meant systematic murder. They discussed the details, such as methods of killing and logistics. None of the men present at the meeting opposed the plan.

The killing of the Jews by the Nazi regime was different from other mass killings in history. The Holocaust was planned. It was intentional. It was not a way to gain land or political advantage. The killing itself was the Nazis' goal. Now, every Jew in Europe faced a deadly threat from the Nazis.

# DEPORTATIONS

By 1941, the Jews in German-controlled lands had already been rounded up and confined to ghettos. Now, the Nazis began deportations to concentration camps. Beginning in late 1941 and lasting through 1944, trains carried humans in cattle cars from every part of the Third Reich to concentration camps.

**Deportation trains usually carried between 1,000 and 2,000 people. The weight of so many people slowed the trains' speed to about 30 miles per hour.**

Ghetto residents head toward the trains that will take them to Chelmno death camp.

photo credit: United States Holocaust Memorial Museum

In some areas, the deportations took place slowly. First, old people were taken, then those who could not work. Later, children and people without family connections left on the trains. Often, Nazis forced the ghetto's Judenrat to choose who would be deported. Not being chosen was only a temporary reprieve. Most Jews were eventually deported from the ghettos.

The Nazis attempted to hide the real purpose of deportation, calling it "resettlement in the East." Those being sent on the trains were told to pack their personal belongings. Clinging to hope, they boarded the trains believing that they were headed to a new home and a fresh start.

The train rides were often unbearably long. Trains from Hungary traveled for days, while trains from Greece took more than a week. In the summer, the cattle cars were stifling hot. In the winter, they were freezing cold. There was little food or water, and sometimes just a bucket for human waste. The train cars were often so crowded that passengers had to stand or sit in human waste. In these close quarters, the stench quickly became overwhelming. By the time the train reached its destination, the passengers spilled out of the cars, exhausted and convinced that they had survived the worst of the trip. Many died on the ride itself. Those who survived the trip were often weak and sick.

## THE KILLING CENTERS

Beginning in 1933, the Nazis began setting up concentration camps throughout the Third Reich. Eventually, there were more than 20,000 camps scattered throughout German-controlled land in Europe. The Nazis first built the camps to hold political opponents and other "undesirables."

> The purpose of the concentration camps changed as Nazi needs changed during World War II.

Some became transit camps, while others held prisoners of war. Some became forced labor camps, while others held women and children. Within a few months of the Wannsee Conference, six of the camps became the killing centers, where large numbers of Jews and other Nazi victims were murdered.

In 1942, concentration camps held about 100,000 prisoners. By January 1945, they held 714,000 people. More than 3 million people, mostly Jews, were murdered in the concentration camps. Some died from starvation, neglect, and brutal conditions. Others were shot or beaten to death. Many more were killed by gassing.

Beginning in 1942, extermination of the Jewish race became the official policy of the Nazi regime. Thousands of people a day were murdered in each of the main killing centers where they carried out this policy: Chelmno, Treblinka, Sobibor, Belzec, Majdanek, and Auschwitz-Birkenau. Most of the killing centers were located near major railroad lines, so that the victims could be transported by train to the centers.

Upon arrival at a death camp, the guards divided the Jews according to their ability to walk. Those who could not walk were taken away and immediately killed. Those who could walk were sent to their first selection. An SS officer pointed for them to move left or right. Old people, pregnant women, young children, and the sick were selected for death. They were segregated by sex before entering the "showers," which were really gas chambers.

## BEAR WITNESS ✡

At each camp, the Nazis gassed victims using either carbon monoxide or Zyklon B, an insecticide that could kill 2,000 people in less than 30 minutes.

## MOBILE GAS VANS

At the Chelmno killing center, mobile gas vans were used to kill Jews beginning in December 1941. The Nazis loaded victims into the vans and killed them with carbon monoxide exhaust fumes. After death, they unloaded and burned the bodies. However, vans could not handle large numbers of victims and SS officials complained that unloading the vans was time-consuming and unpleasant.

At Auschwitz, prisoners were subjected to medical experimentation. Air force physician Dr. Horst Schumann carried out sterilization experiments in which he irradiated the reproductive organs of male and female prisoners.

Dr. Josef Mengele experimented on Romani children, twins, dwarfs, and people with physical disabilities. The prisoners endured all sorts of medical analysis and testing while they were alive. Some subjects were killed by injection so that their internal organs could be autopsied and studied. Mengele's goal was to prove the superiority of the Aryan race.

Those selected for death often had no idea what lay ahead of them. Guards instructed them to remove their clothing because they were going to be showered and deloused. Signs at the entrance of the gas chamber said "Baths and Disinfecting Rooms" to keep up the deception. Once they had undressed, guards led them into the gas chamber.

The gas chambers could hold hundreds of people at a time. Fake shower heads tricked victims into believing that they were really in a shower. Once the final inmate entered, guards quickly locked and sealed the doors. They discharged poison gas through vents in the ceilings. The people closest to the vents usually died immediately. Those farther away lasted a few minutes longer. Within 20 to 30 minutes, all were dead. After about 30 minutes, ventilators sucked the poisonous gas from the room.

Once the gassing was finished, work units of other camp prisoners, called Sonderkommandos, entered the chamber and removed the bodies. They extracted any gold teeth from the victims' mouths and transported the bodies to the crematorium.

## SLAVE LABOR

Those not immediately selected for death at the camps were given numbers, which was sewn onto their uniforms. Guards called prisoners by their numbers, not their names. Prisoners also wore other cloth badges to identify where they came from and why they were at camp.

Many of these prisoners were forced into slave labor. As World War II progressed, the Germans needed laborers to produce goods for the war effort. The concentration camps became a source of forced labor.

Most of the work was hard, physical labor. Some inmates worked in factories for German companies. Working conditions for camp prisoners were brutal. Prisoners often worked 11-hour shifts with little food. Workers died by the thousands, only to be replaced by a new group of incoming prisoners.

## AUSCHWITZ-BIRKENAU

Opened in June 1940, Auschwitz-Birkenau was the largest of the Nazi death camps. Located in Oswiecim, Poland, it was actually three camps. Auschwitz was a concentration camp, Birkenau was a killing center, and Monowitz was a complex of slave-labor camps. More than a million people were killed at Auschwitz. That's more than at any other camp.

Auschwitz-Birkenau, summer 1944

photo credit: Yad Vashem

As soon as prisoners arrived at Auschwitz-Birkenau, they were selected for work or death. Healthy men were picked for work, while women, children, and the elderly were often sent to immediate death. Families were split up. Most never saw each other again.

Those selected for work were stripped of their personal clothing. They were shaved and tattooed with identifying numbers. Those new to the camp were also sprayed with disinfectant and forced into scalding hot showers, all in an attempt to reduce infection.

Each prisoner was given a uniform with their number sewn onto it. They were measured and logged into the camp records. Some had photos taken. Clothing, valuables, and other personal belongings were confiscated and taken to warehouses. The prisoners slept in wooden barracks that housed hundreds of prisoners, crowded on planks of wood with no pillows or mattresses.

Prisoners in the concentration camp at Sachsenhausen, Germany, December 19, 1938

photo credit: National Archives

> In the cramped and unsanitary conditions of the camps, contagious diseases such as typhus, typhoid fever, tuberculosis, and dysentery spread quickly, killing many prisoners.

Jakob Blankitny was a Polish Jew who was sent to Auschwitz at age 16. Blankitny was the only member of his family to survive the Holocaust. He remembers the horrific conditions in the following essay.

"It was winter and the cold burned us; all the camp was flooded and muddy. They took our winter clothes and in exchange, gave us light clothes that looked like striped pajamas. With time you could see through these clothes, the extreme state of malnutrition and weakness of our bodies. They placed us in different barracks, with three-story bunks, placing four people per bed; totaling twelve humans per bunk. Our life in the camp started at five o'clock in the morning when they gave us coffee and a piece of bread. At the same time, we were counted like animals; making sure that nobody was missing. We were beaten and abused constantly, especially if someone unfortunately fell or moved in place because of the hard beatings. These beatings were executed at that immediate instant; making the vile SS soldiers fill with laughter to see in our faces, the horror to which we were subjected."

The horrors of the killing camps lasted throughout World War II. But what about after the war? What happened when Germany and the Axis powers lost to the Allies? We'll look at the events following World War II in the next chapter.

In addition to Jews, the concentration camps held victims from other groups who were also persecuted by the Nazis. These included Soviet prisoners of war, political prisoners, common criminals, Romani people, and homosexuals.

## KEY QUESTIONS

- Why didn't any country stop the German Nazis from killing so many people?

- Do you think the Holocaust could happen again? How can we ensure that it doesn't?

# POETRY OF THE HOLOCAUST

Jews living in ghettos and concentration camps resisted the Nazis in one of the only ways that they could. They attempted to preserve Jewish history and the life of Jews even as the Nazis worked to erase the Jewish people and their memory from Europe. As part of these efforts, Jewish people wrote poetry. Some wrote poems during the Holocaust, while others wrote in the years afterward. They used their poetry to express a variety of experiences and feelings about the Holocaust.

---

* **You can read some examples of Holocaust poetry here.**

🔍 Holocaust Memorial Day Trust

* **Choose a Holocaust poem to read and analyze.**

  * What do you think the poet is trying to convey in this poem?

  * What experiences or feelings have they written about?

  * Is the poem more hopeful and optimistic or more dark and pessimistic? Explain.

  * How does the poem make you think about the Holocaust?

> To investigate more, imagine that you are a Holocaust survivor. Create your own piece of Holocaust poetry to document your journey.

# Chapter 5 ▶
# War's End

Was the end of
the war the end of
the Holocaust?

While the systematic murdering of Jews and other people stopped when the war ended, there was still much to be done to save the millions of sick and displaced people within Germany and German-occupied lands.

||||||||||||||||||||||||||||||||||||||||||||||||||||||

By the winter of 1944–45, the Germans knew they were losing the war. Allied armies advanced on two fronts: the Soviets from the east and the Americans and British from the west.

SS officials ordered the evacuation of death camps in the paths of advancing Allied troops. In an attempt to conceal the evidence of mass murder, they dismantled the camps. They forced the camps' prisoners to march toward Germany. Why? They did not want to leave any eyewitnesses to their crimes.

## DEATH MARCHES

The death marches forced on thousands of prisoners from the concentration camps toward Germany served three purposes. First, SS officials did not want prisoners to be able to tell their stories to Allied forces. They also believed that they needed the prisoners as slave labor to continue producing war goods for the German army.

Finally, some SS officials believed that they might be able to use Jewish prisoners as hostages. They needed something to bargain with, to make a deal with the Allies that would allow the survival of the Nazi regime.

The first camp evacuations in 1944 were often carried out by train or ship. With winter approaching, SS officials increasingly evacuated concentration camp prisoners on foot, sometimes making them walk hundreds of miles.

Remember, these prisoners had suffered greatly at the camps and were not in good health. During the march, prisoners were given very little food, water, or rest. As they walked, the prisoners were treated harshly by the SS guards. They shot hundreds who collapsed or could not keep up.

[
Thousands of prisoners died
from starvation, exhaustion, and
exposure on the death marches.
]

In November 1944, tens of thousands of Hungarian Jews marched to the Austrian border. Those who survived were sent to Dachau and Mauthausen concentration camps. In January 1945, 66,000 prisoners marched from Auschwitz to Wodzislaw, where they boarded freight trains to concentration camps in Germany. One in four died on the trip.

The Nazis had spent years deporting Jews to the east and sending them out of Germany to killing centers. The death marches moved them back into Germany.

## HERMANN GÖRING (1893–1946)

Another influential member of the Nazi Party was Hermann Göring. He organized and formed the Gestapo, the Nazi state security police. Göring served as Hitler's second-in-command and oversaw economic programs, military expansion, and other important policies. In 1935, he was named commander of the German air force, the Luftwaffe. In 1938, Göring ordered the exclusion of Jews from German society and economy. In July 1941, he issued the order to initiate a "Final Solution to the Jewish Question," the Nazi's plan to exterminate all Jews. Göring committed suicide after being convicted of war crimes and crimes against humanity at the Nuremberg trials in 1945.

# LIBERATION BEGINS

A survivor named Lilly Appelbaum described a death march from Auschwitz to Bergen-Belsen.

*"Word came to us that we were going to evacuate Auschwitz. . . . And so we . . . we all walked out [of] Auschwitz and we started walking. And we started walking, we walked for days. . . . And as we walked we heard gun shots and they told us to keep on marching. We heard gun shots and they were shooting people in the back who couldn't keep up with the walking. It ended up being called the death march because the ravines and the gutters, they were all red from blood."*

On July 23, 1944, Soviet soldiers entered Majdanek concentration camp outside Lublin, Poland. As the army moved closer, the camp's SS guards unsuccessfully tried to hide, burn, and bury the evidence of their crimes. Because of the quick Soviet advance, the Nazis did not have time to complete their evacuation efforts.

When the Soviet soldiers entered the camp, they discovered a few prisoners who reported what had happened at the camp. The Soviets also found other evidence of SS crimes, including a warehouse of 800,000 pairs of shoes taken from the camp's victims. Even soldiers who were battle hardened by war were shocked at what they found.

During the summer of 1944, Soviet troops entered the killing centers of Belzec, Treblinka, and Sobibor. The centers had been closed the year before and turned into farms. Now Soviet soldiers found human bones sticking out from the ground.

On January 27, 1945, Soviet troops entered Auschwitz. The Nazis had already evacuated most of the camp's 67,000 prisoners on death marches. Those who remained were too sick to walk. Before they left, the SS attempted to hide the activity at Auschwitz. They blew up crematoria buildings and destroyed SS documents. Storerooms holding Jewish clothing and personal property were burned.

British troops liberated the Bergen-Belsen concentration camp on April 15, 1945. A disease called typhus had ravaged the camp and thousands of bodies lay rotting on the ground. About 60,000 prisoners were found alive, although many of them were in desperate condition. More than 14,000 died within the first weeks of freedom.

Appalled at what they found, the British troops brought local civilians into the camp and showed them the horrors. The British also filmed what they found and broadcast the films for the world to witness.

On April 11, 1945, American troops entered Buchenwald, one of the largest concentration camps, located near Weimar, Germany. A few days before they arrived, the SS had marched 25,000 prisoners out of the camp. The few remaining prisoners greeted the Americans on their arrival.

The Americans liberated several other camps in April and May of 1945, including Dachau on April 29, 1945. As the Americans neared the camp, they approached cautiously because they expected a fight from SS guards. As they got closer, they found train boxcars filled with dead bodies. The sight of so much death stirred the Americans and they rushed toward the camp. Once they arrived, they turned over the SS guards to the prisoners for judgment.

## KEEPING RECORD

Some people kept records of the events of the Holocaust for as long as they were able. You can read eyewitness accounts of Jews being deported at these websites.

Eva Heyman deportations from the Ghetto

Survivor Edi Weinstein bartering for water

Child survivors of Auschwitz

A member of the U.S. Army's 70th Armored Infantry, Dallas Peyton of Tucson, Arizona, entered Dachau camp with other liberating soldiers. He recalls what he saw there.

*"I remember a couple of scenes very vivid. One, when we were approaching, we saw a trainload of prisoners. Turned out they were not prisoners. It was a trainload of bodies that had been sent to Dachau from Buchenwald, I presume to be, to go through the furnaces, ovens, of Dachau. . . . The other scene was in the camp grounds. I saw two of these living walking skeletons shuffling along toward each other. They got within a few yards of each other, stopped, stared at each other, and then they tried to run, and embraced. They were either related or very close friends, and until that moment neither knew the other was still alive. And yet they'd been in that same prison for who knows how long."*

The Allies liberated the last concentration camps in May 1945. At last, the Holocaust was over. Days later, the war was over. The recovery from the war's devastation, however, would last for decades. At each camp they liberated, the Allies encountered horrific conditions and piles of bodies. Forced labor, lack of food, and months of maltreatment left the few survivors so weak they could barely move. Many looked more like skeletons than human beings. Already weak, many survivors fell victim to disease. Rescuers burned many of the camps to prevent the spread of contagious disease.

> Those who were lucky enough to survive the camps now faced a long, difficult recovery.

## HITLER'S RETREAT

In April 1945, as Allied forces approached Berlin, Hitler retreated to an underground air-raid shelter in the Reich Chancellery. Reports show that Hitler was unable to sleep and feared being taken prisoner by the Allies. Some of Hitler's staff fled the city.

In his final hours in the shelter, Hitler married his long-time girlfriend, Eva Braun. Then he dictated his last words. He named a new president and chancellor. He also charged the leaders of Reich and all of their loyal followers to observe the Nazi race laws and to be unwavering in their opposition to the Jews, who he declared to be the "universal poisoner of all peoples."

In the shelter, Eva Braun committed suicide by taking poison. Rather than being captured by the Allies, Hitler shot himself. The Third Reich died with him.

# HUMANITARIAN CRISIS

With the liberation of the concentration camps, the world faced an enormous humanitarian crisis. Military chaplains and relief workers stepped in to help the survivors. One of the relief workers' first priorities was to establish feeding programs for the starving survivors. Some survivors were so weak, they could not feed themselves. Nurses had to spoon feed them. Many survivors suffered severe psychological problems.

Disease was another major problem. Rodents and bugs infested the camps and spread diseases from person to person. Many survivors had lice and bacterial infections. Aid workers sprayed the camps and survivors with disinfectants to prevent further spread of disease. Doctors and nurses examined the survivors and determined what treatments they needed to regain their health.

Soldiers also faced another immediate problem—bodies lay scattered around the camps, rotting in the open. To prevent more disease, the troops buried the bodies in mass graves.

# DISPLACED PERSONS

When the Allied troops liberated Europe from Nazi control in 1944 and 1945, up to 9 million people were living in countries not their own. About 6 million returned to their native countries. Others refused to return because they feared retaliation from their countrymen or persecution from new Communist governments in Eastern Europe. Many Jewish survivors did not have a home to which they could return. The Nazis had stripped them of citizenship and their property in Germany and German-occupied lands.

## BEAR WITNESS ✡

More than 1 million children were killed during the Holocaust.

## AFTERMATH

The Allied soldiers were determined that the German people should see firsthand the devastation brought by the Nazis. They brought local citizens from surrounding communities and gave them tours of the concentration camps. They pressed some German civilians to help the clean-up efforts by digging graves and burying the dead. Why do you think it was important to the Allied soldiers that German citizens see the concentration camps? How might the sight of the dead bodies and sick inmates affect them?

As the Jews returned to the homes and neighborhoods they'd been driven from, many of the locals treated them with hostility because they feared that the Jews would demand the return of property and belongings.

## BACK TO LIFE

The refugee camps elected committees to run the camp. These committees improved sanitation and hygiene. They established schools, farms, and religious centers. As things slowly improved, survivors began to rebuild their lives. They married and formed new families.

Mothers who had lost children during the Holocaust gave birth to new babies.

When the war ended, Jewish survivors did not have any papers or passports. During the Holocaust, their communities had been destroyed or taken over by strangers. They had nowhere to go.

Many Jewish displaced persons went to refugee centers and camps set up on the sites of former concentration camps. The Allies set up these camps across Austria, Italy, and Germany. The United Nations Relief and Rehabilitation Administration and the American, British, and French armies ran these camps.

The camps were overcrowded and there never seemed to be enough food. For many displaced people, living in these camps meant staying in Germany along with the same Germans who had stood by and allowed the Nazis to terrorize, torture, and murder them and their family and friends. Eventually, Jewish displaced people were allowed to stay in separate camps. As time went on, life inside the refugee camps began to improve for the Holocaust survivors.

# A PERMANENT HOME

Despite small signs of progress and hope, life in the refugee camps was only temporary. The Jews wanted a new place to begin a permanent life. Finding a home was not easy. For many, it took years to resettle in a new place. Many European countries closed their borders to homeless, displaced people.

At the same time, immigration quotas in the United States still restricted the number of Jews who could move to America. On December 22, 1945, President Harry Truman loosened restrictions for people displaced by the Nazis. In 1948, Congress also passed the Displaced Persons Act. It provided immigration visas for about 400,000 people between 1949 and 1952, about 68,000 of which were Jewish.

Schoolchildren at Schauenstein displaced persons camp, c. 1946

Many Jews wanted to start their lives again in Palestine. They wanted to create a Jewish homeland, near the same lands where the Jewish people had lived centuries earlier. In 1944, the Jewish Brigade Group formed to help Jewish refugees relocate to Palestine. Jews already living in Palestine organized for some refugees to travel there by ship. British officials turned away most of the ships and detained and denied entry to the Jewish refugees.

In 1947, the United Nations General Assembly voted to split Palestine into two new states, one Arab and the other Jewish. In 1948, the State of Israel was established. It was the first Jewish state to be created in 2,000 years. Jewish displaced persons flocked to the new country. By 1953, as many as 170,000 Jewish refugees had immigrated to Israel. Other refugees emigrated to Canada, Australia, New Zealand, Mexico, South America, and South Africa. In 1953, the last Jewish displaced persons camp in Germany closed.

Now that the Holocaust was over, the world had a very important question to ask—how could it have happened in the first place?

**PS**

**KEY QUESTIONS**

- How did the world handle the humanitarian crisis of millions of displaced people after World War II? Do you think there was a better way?

- Why was there disagreement about allowing Jews to settle permanently in Jerusalem?

# FINDING FAMILY

Throughout the Holocaust, families were separated and often had no information about what had happened to their loved ones. After the Holocaust ended, survivors began the difficult task of searching for family members. Jewish organizations created registries, where survivors could register and search for family. The International Red Cross and Jewish relief organizations set up tracing services to help with the search, but with millions of displaced people throughout Europe, the search was often long and difficult. Survivors also placed newspaper notices, hoping for information about their family. Some lucky people were reunited with family quickly. For many, the search took years and ended with the discovery that they were the only members of their family to survive.

---

## VOCAB LAB

Write down what you think each of the following words means. What root words can you find for help?

**death march, hostage, maltreatment, humanitarian, displaced person, refugee center, hygiene, visa,** and **State of Israel.**

Compare your definitions with those of your friends or classmates. Did you all come up with the same meanings? Turn to the text and glossary if you need help.

- **Imagine that you are a survivor searching for your parents after the Holocaust.**

  - Without any documents or photographs of your family, how would you go about finding them?

  - What identifying details could you use to help locate your family?

- **Using this information, create a newspaper notice or other search tool to find your family.**

---

To investigate more, consider that today, people looking for friends and relatives can use the Internet to quickly send messages to a large number of people over a wide distance. How would the search for missing family be different if the Internet had existed during the Holocaust? In what ways would it have changed how people searched for their families?

# Chapter 6 ▶
# How Could the Holocaust Happen?

How did the rest of the world react to stories of the Holocaust during the war?

Most countries ignored the evidence that mass murder was being committed by the Nazis. Most countries refused to help the Jews who were trying to escape brutal mistreatment and possible death.

After the Holocaust was over, many people wondered how it could have happened. For years, the world stood by and did little while the Nazis persecuted and murdered the Jewish people across occupied Europe. How did people around the world fail to recognize the Nazi genocide and stop it before it was too late?

Early on, the Nazis tried to think of ways to rid Germany of its Jews. Initially, they favored a policy of forced emigration. Jews were allowed, even encouraged, to leave Germany and to take some money and personal belongings with them. At first, many Jews were reluctant to leave their homes. However, as Nazi persecution intensified and more civil and personal rights were stripped away from them, many Jews decided to leave Germany. When Germany annexed Austria in 1938, an additional 185,000 Jews fell under Nazi control. Those who wanted to leave faced a difficult problem—where could they go?

> As the number of Jews looking to leave Germany and Nazi-controlled lands increased, other countries grew more unwilling to accept them for various economic and social reasons.

**By 1938, as many as 150,000 Jews had left Germany. But many more were unable to leave.**

## EVIAN CONFERENCE

In July 1938, delegates from 32 countries met at the Evian Conference in Evian, France, to discuss the Jewish refugee crisis. U.S. President Franklin D. Roosevelt called for the conference in response to mounting pressure to do something about the Jewish refugees.

For nine days, the delegates discussed the refugee problem. They expressed their sympathy for the situation of the Jews. At the same time, each gave excuses as to why their country could not take in more Jewish refugees. Britain explained that it was only a small island. It refused to open British-controlled Palestine to Jewish refugees. Recovering from the Great Depression, the United States declined to remove limits on its immigration policies.

In response to the Evian Conference, the German Foreign Office issued a statement, noting the hypocrisy of the countries involved:

> "Since in many countries it was recently regarded as wholly incomprehensible why Germany did not wish to preserve in its population an element like the Jews . . . it appears astounding that countries seem in no way anxious to make use of these elements themselves now that the opportunity offers."

**BEAR WITNESS** ✡

A few countries did offer help. Holland and Denmark extended temporary asylum for a few Jewish refugees. And the Dominican Republic offered to accept 100,000 Jewish refugees, although few Jews went to the Caribbean nation.

# LIMITS ON IMMIGRATION

After the violence of Kristallnacht in 1938, the Jews realized that they could no longer live safely in Germany. Many who had chosen to stay, now tried desperately to leave. But there were few places they could go. After World War I, Britain controlled Palestine in the Middle East. However, because the Arab nations in the region opposed Jewish immigration, the British restricted the number of Jewish immigrants it would allow.

In the United States, a strict quota system limited the number of immigrants based on their country of origin. To obtain a visa for entry, a prospective immigrant had to fill out many forms and submit them to the American consulates in Europe. The consulate issued visas, but only rarely. A long list of requirements disqualified many applicants, such as if an applicant did not have enough money. Applicants also needed to obtain a certificate of good conduct from their local police, a task that was increasingly difficult for Jews in Germany, where the police force was controlled by the Nazis.

Americans waiting to receive relief checks from the government during the Great Depression

photo credit: Dorothea Lange

After World War II began, German Jews were denied entry on the basis that they might be spies. The visa process was so selective that, between 1933 and 1945, the quotas for immigrants from Germany and Austria were filled during only two of those years, 1938 and 1939.

Although the United States had a history of welcoming persecuted people, many people in the United States were reluctant to welcome Jewish refugees. Anti-Semitism was still widespread through the country.

> In addition, the country was recovering from the Great Depression.

Americans feared that opening the country to immigrants would take away scarce jobs from American families that were already struggling. According to public opinion polls in 1938 and 1939, 95 percent of Americans disapproved of the Nazi regime, but less than 9 percent wanted to allow more refugees into the country.

Even efforts to rescue children were met with resistance. In February 1939, the Wagner-Rogers Bill was introduced in Congress to grant special permission for 20,000 German children to come to the United States. The bill stated that the children would be supported by private citizens and organizations, not the government. However, opponents of the bill argued that American children should be taken care of first. Other groups argued that it was designed to help only Jewish children instead of all German children. As a result, the Wagner-Rogers Bill never came to the floor of the House of Representatives or the Senate for a vote.

## LITTLE INFORMATION

The Nazis took great effort to conceal the details of the Holocaust from the rest of world. In the 1930s and '40s, there was no Internet and most homes still did not have a television for news. People relied on newspapers and radio broadcasts to hear the latest updates on the war in Europe. However, stories about Nazi persecution and murder of Jews rarely made the headlines and were instead relegated to the newspapers' back pages or to brief radio updates. While movie theaters showed short news films before feature films, the news films were mainly about the war and rarely mentioned the Holocaust. Without the full story, people around the world did not understand the desperate situation facing the Jews in Europe.

# NO PLACE FOR THE *ST. LOUIS*

On May 13, 1939, a luxury liner, the *S.S. St. Louis*, sailed from Germany carrying 937 passengers, mostly Jews. The ship headed to Cuba. Armed with landing permits, the passengers were filled with hope for new beginnings and relief at escaping the increasing brutalism in Nazi Germany.

When the ship reached the Havana port on May 27, the Cuban government refused to accept the passengers' landing permits. Unbeknownst to the passengers, a week before the ship left Germany, the Cuban president had invalidated the landing permits. As the ship sat in the Havana harbor, the passengers were not allowed to disembark.

The Cubans offered to allow the passengers to land if they paid a bribe of $1 million. The American Jewish Joint Distribution Committee (JDC) appealed to the U.S. State Department on behalf of the refugees. Passengers themselves sent a telegram to President Roosevelt asking for help. The White House remained silent.

The JDC reached out to other nearby countries to see if they would accept the passengers of the *St. Louis*. None agreed. As the ship left Havana's harbor, it sailed along the Florida coast, in full view of Miami's lights. U.S. Coast Guard ships patrolled the shoreline to make sure no passengers tried to jump from the ship and swim to shore. Unwelcome in every port, the ship turned back to Europe.

Upon its return, Belgium, the Netherlands, England, and France agreed to admit the refugees. Months later, the German army invaded most of these countries. Only the 288 passengers who went to England were safe. The rest were back under Nazi control.

Jewish refugees look out a porthole aboard the *St. Louis*. They don't know yet that they'll be refused entrance.

PS

# COLLABORATION

During the Holocaust, the Nazis were helped by other leaders and governments who cooperated with the occupiers. Motivated by anti-Semitism, nationalism, anti-communism, and fear, the citizens in German-occupied lands collaborated with the Nazi regime and their racial policies. Collaboration with the Nazis took place in every country occupied by Germans.

In some Axis countries, military groups terrorized, robbed, and murdered Jewish citizens. In Slovakia, Romania, Croatia, and Hungary, local guards were responsible for the deaths of thousands of Jews.

In France, the Vichy government cooperated with the Nazis by passing laws that defined Jews by race and restricted their rights. Vichy authorities also established internment camps in southern France. They arrested Jews and helped deport Jews to killing centers in Poland.

> Of the 75,000 French Jews who were deported, only about 2,500 survived.

In Norway, police and paramilitary forces helped the SS and German police deport Jews to Auschwitz-Birkenau. In Belgium, local officials helped gather and deport Jewish citizens. They created a national register of Jews and turned it over to the Nazis. Local groups carried out anti-Semitic campaigns. When the Nazis occupied the Netherlands, the government helped them by taking away Jewish rights. They, too, assisted the Germans in deporting Jews to killing centers.

## BEAR WITNESS ✡

Collaborators helped round up Jews for deportation to killing centers and even participated in the actual killing.

## EASTERN EUROPE

In Eastern Europe, collaborators took a more active role in helping the Nazis carry out their destruction of the Jews. In Estonia, Latvia, Lithuania, and the Ukraine, collaborators served as perimeter guards in killing centers and were involved in the gassing of hundreds of thousands of prisoners. Lithuanian military units worked with the SS to murder thousands of Jews. Others served as auxiliaries for German police forces and military units.

# MISSED OPPORTUNITIES

Time after time, the world missed clues and opportunities to fully recognize Nazi intentions and intervene before millions died. In 1942, Gerhart Riegner, a World Jewish Congress official in Geneva, Switzerland, tried to warn the U.S. and British governments about the planned Nazi Holocaust.

In July, he received a phone call from a friend who reported that a German industrialist had revealed a plan to exterminate all the Jews in Europe. Riegner sent telegrams to the U.S. and British officials warning them of the plan to annihilate the Jews. Riegner's telegram was the first authoritative word that the Nazis had a coordinated plan to kill the Jews.

> It took four months for the United States and the Soviet Union to issue a warning to Germany to stop the Holocaust.

It took 18 months before U.S. President Roosevelt created the War Refugee Board to try to save the Jews. By then, millions had already died.

In 1944, another opportunity to save some of those who would be killed in the Holocaust was missed. Together with Polish resistance, a small group of escaped prisoners from Auschwitz put together a 30-page report known as the Auschwitz Protocol. It detailed the workings of the camp, estimated the number of people killed, and warned of plans to kill hundreds of thousands more. The document also included maps and sketches of the camp that showed the location of the gas chambers and crematoria.

## BLETCHLEY PARK

In Britain's Bletchley Park, also known as Station X, the government's code-breaking center operated during World War II. The center intercepted and decoded German messages. According to documents released after the war, some of the intercepted and decoded messages showed that British leaders knew the Nazis were systematically killing Jews in the Soviet Union beginning in 1941. Yet they did nothing to intervene.

In June 1944, Jewish organizations called on the American government to bomb Auschwitz's gas chambers and the railroad that led to the camp. The U.S. Assistant Secretary of War John McCloy rejected these requests, saying that the bombing was impractical and would divert air forces that were needed elsewhere in the war. Today, historians debate whether bombing Auschwitz would have prevented further murders in the camp's gas chambers.

> [ Reading the history of the Holocaust can be infuriating. ]

How could people stand by and do nothing while others suffered? In fact, there were people working hard and at great risk to help as much as they could. We'll meet some of them in the next chapter.

## VOCAB LAB

Write down what you think each of the following words means. What root words can you find for help?

**paramilitary**, **delegate**, **asylum**, **quota**, **consulate**, **invalidate**, **internment camp**, **register**, and **divert**.

Compare your definitions with those of your friends or classmates. Did you all come up with the same meanings? Turn to the text and glossary if you need help.

## KEY QUESTIONS

- **Many countries claimed economic trouble as a reason to refuse to allow Jews to enter. Do you think racism was another reason?**

- **Do you think the Holocaust could happen in this age, when we have the Internet and social media? Why or why not?**

- **Can you think of immigrant populations that are having trouble finding places to resettle in today's world? Do some research on a current refugee crisis. What is different about their situation? What is similar?**

# TRACE THE FATE OF A PASSENGER ON THE *ST. LOUIS*

In the spring of 1996, the United States Holocaust Memorial Museum began a project to trace the fate of the 937 passengers of the *St. Louis* after they were denied landing in Cuba. The refugees returned to Europe and resettled in England, France, Belgium, and the Netherlands in the summer of 1939.

---

* **To learn more about the ship, you can read an interview with one of the ship's passengers here.**

* **What happened to the passengers?** You can view the full passenger list for the ship at this website.

🔍 St. Louis survivor's story

🔍 St. Louis full passenger list

* **Select a few passengers and trace what happened to them.** You can also research more about individual passengers by reading *Refuge Denied: The St. Louis Passengers and the Holocaust* by Sarah A. Ogilvie and Scott Miller.

  * How did where they ended up resettling when the *St. Louis* returned to Europe affect people's fate?

  * How might their fate have been different if they had been allowed to land in Cuba or the United States?

To investigate more, consider that when the *St. Louis* was refused entry by Cuba, the ship's passengers appealed to U.S. President Roosevelt to allow them to land in the United States. Write a persuasive letter to President Roosevelt asking him to allow the passengers of the *St. Louis* to land on American soil. What arguments will you use in your letter?

# CREATE A POLITICAL CARTOON

A political cartoon is a cartoon that makes a point about a political issue or event. Today, political cartoons are in newspapers, usually on the editorial pages. While these cartoons can be funny, they are meant to make you think about current events and persuade you to agree with the cartoonist's point of view. Cartoonists use several methods to persuade people, including symbolism, exaggeration, labeling, and irony.

* **Think about your reaction to the story of the** *S.S. St. Louis* **and its passengers.** Do you agree with the countries that denied them entry? Do you think they should have been allowed to disembark?

* **Look at some political cartoons.** Then create a political cartoon that reflects your views on the issue of the *St. Louis*. Show people your cartoon and observe their reactions.

  * What techniques will you use to persuade people to agree with your opinion?

  * What is their reaction?

  * Do they react the way you intended? Why or why not?

> To investigate more, create another cartoon that shows the reaction of the U.S. government to the *St. Louis* passengers' pleas for help. What will you include? What might you leave out?

# SPEAK AT THE EVIAN CONFERENCE

At the Evian Conference, delegates from several countries discussed the Jewish refugee problem. Many explained why their country could not accept more Jewish refugees. Others, such as the Dominican Republic, offered sanctuary to thousands of Jews.

- **Imagine that you have been invited to speak to the delegates at the conference on behalf of the Jewish refugees.** Prepare a persuasive speech to convince the countries to change their immigration laws or quotas. Use the Internet and primary sources to research your speech. As you write your speech, consider the following.

  - What logical arguments will you make to persuade countries to accept more immigrants?

  - What facts and statistics will you use to support your arguments?

  - How will you use emotional appeals to convince your audience?

  - Will you use an attention-grabbing device to begin your speech?

> To investigate more, research today's immigration policies. What do immigrants need to do to be able to move to the United States? How have these policies changed since the 1930s? How do you think they will change in the future as issues such as terrorism and civil war continue to affect the global community?

# Chapter 7

# Rescue and Resistance

Why did some individuals and groups put themselves at risk to help Jewish people?

Many people felt they could not stand by and watch while the Nazis persecuted, tortured, and killed innocents. They worked to find a way to help, even as they put themselves in danger by doing so.

While millions of people stood silently as the Nazis persecuted the Jews and others, some individuals and groups risked their lives to help. They helped in many different ways. Some provided hiding places for Jewish refugees or led them to underground escape routes. Others provided Jews with false papers, food, clothing, money, and weapons.

Some acted on their own, while others coordinated their efforts with larger groups of people. Sometimes entire communities worked together to save the Jews from Nazi persecution.

Different motivations drove these people to action. Some sympathized with the Jewish people and did not believe in persecution based on religion. Others were anti-Semitic, but could not condone murder and genocide. Some helped personal friends who happened to be Jews, while others aided total strangers.

Every day, these rescuers put their lives at risk to save others. Even so, most insisted that their actions were not heroic. They simply did what needed to be done to help others in a time of desperate need.

# RESCUING THE JEWS OF DENMARK

Unlike many other countries in Europe, Denmark had a long history of tolerance toward its Jewish citizens. Danish Jews were accepted into society and treated like any other Danish citizens. Even when the Germans occupied most of Europe, including Denmark, the Danish Jews were not persecuted by local citizens.

In 1943, as the Germans carried out their Final Solution, Danish leaders learned of the planned deportation of Jews from Denmark. Danish officials took the warning seriously and quickly moved to sneak their Jewish citizens out of the country before they could be deported to one of the German death camps. People from all parts of Danish society, including fishermen, farmers, businessmen, doctors, and clergy, joined together to coordinate the evacuation. The Jewish rabbis told their communities to go into hiding. Jews left the Danish cities on foot or by train, car, and taxi. They hid in private homes, hospitals, churches, and farms. Then, they fled Denmark by sea.

In October 1943, more than 7,000 Jews left Denmark on fishing boats. Danish police helped the rescue effort, while the coast guard escorted the boats. For two weeks, the fishing boats carried Jews from Denmark to Sweden, which was a neutral country. In Sweden, the Jews found a safe haven. Because of these efforts, more than 90 percent of Jews in Denmark escaped being sent to Nazi death camps.

The Danish people also protected the property of Jewish refugees. They inventoried Jewish homes and possessions and put their businesses in trusts. Holy objects were stored in churches and returned to the Jewish community after the war ended.

## BEAR WITNESS ✡

In France, Belgium, and Italy, underground networks run by Catholic priests and nuns and Catholic citizens saved thousands of Jews. These networks hid and smuggled Jews to safety in Switzerland and Spain.

## ZEGOTA RESISTANCE

In Poland, some Polish people risked their own safety to help the Jews. "Zegota" was the code name for the Council to Aid the Jews. It was a Polish underground organization that helped Jews by finding them safe hiding places, money, or false identity papers. Some members of Zegota helped the Jews because of their personal friendships, while others opposed persecution based on religion. Some simply could not support mass murder.

Irena Sendler, a Polish Catholic social worker, was an early activist in Zegota. As a senior official in Warsaw's welfare department, she used her position to gain access to the ghetto. She set up a network to organize escapes and provide false documents.

> She helped to smuggle thousands of children out of the Warsaw Ghetto to safety.

She hid them in ambulances. To distract Nazi guards in case one of the children cried, she kept a barking dog in the front seat.

Using her contacts at orphanages and convents, Sendler arranged to get the Jewish children to safety, often under new Christian names. She kept records of the children and their parents written on tissue paper and buried in jars under an apple tree so that they would not be found by the Gestapo, the Nazi secret police.

In 1943, the Gestapo arrested Sendler and sent her to prison, where she was tortured. A bribed guard helped her escape and she remained in hiding for the rest of the war while she continued working for Zegota.

### SAFE HAVEN IN LE CHAMBON-SUR-LIGNON

In the south of France, the village of Le Chambon-sur-Lignon became a haven for about 5,000 Jews. Many of the people who lived in the town were French Protestants whose ancestors had been persecuted in France by Roman Catholics. They built a network of villagers who sheltered Jews in their homes and on their farms. Local Catholic convents and monasteries also helped with the rescue.

Years later, when asked about their actions, the citizens of Le Chambon did not accept praise. Instead, they explained that they were simply doing what had to be done. Why do you think they refused to be praised for their actions?

# KINDERTRANSPORT

A series of rescue efforts known as Kindertransport, saved thousands of Jewish children between 1938 and 1940. After the violence of Kristallnacht in November 1938, the British government reduced immigration restrictions for certain types of Jewish refugees. They agreed to let children under the age of 17 enter Great Britain from Germany, Austria, and Czechoslovakia. Each child had to be sponsored by private citizens or organizations, which guaranteed payment for their care, education, and emigration to Britain.

The British government then allowed these children to enter Britain on temporary travel visas. When the crisis in Germany was over, the children were to return to their homes and families. Parents and other adults were not allowed to come with the children.

The first Kindertransport arrived in Great Britain on December 2, 1938, carrying about 200 children from a Berlin orphanage. The children traveled by train to ports in Belgium and the Netherlands. From there, they sailed to Great Britain. Some children boarded a plane directly to Britain from Czechoslovakia. The last transport from Germany left on September 1, 1939, as World War II began. In the Netherlands, the last transport sailed for Britain on May 14, 1940, before the Dutch fell to the German invasion.

Once they arrived in Britain, children with sponsors traveled to London to meet their foster families. Children without sponsors lived at a summer camp and other facilities until a family agreed to take them.

The Kindertransport rescued about 9,000 to 10,000 children from Germany. After the war, many of these children became citizens of Great Britain. Others emigrated to Israel, the United States, Canada, and Australia. Most never saw their families again.

**Jewish organizations inside Germany planned the transport of children out of the country. They often chose children who were homeless, orphans, or whose parents were in concentration camps.**

## BEAR WITNESS ✡

Rescuers came from every religious background—Protestant and Catholic, Eastern Orthodox and Muslim.

# OSKAR SCHINDLER

Many individuals risked their lives to save others during the Holocaust. An ethnic German and a Catholic, Oskar Schindler owned several factories near Krakow, Poland. At one of his factories, he employed Jewish workers who lived in the nearby Krakow Ghetto. Later, he hired prisoners from the Krakow-Plaszow concentration camp.

Schindler got to know many of the employees and often ordered extra soup rations for them. When the Nazis began deporting Jews to killing centers in 1943, Schindler approached the German government and received permission to build a barracks on his factory property.

He convinced them that it would make the factory more efficient and save time on the workers' commute to and from the ghetto. In reality, this arrangement allowed his workers to escape the ghetto and deportation.

[ If caught in this deception, Schindler could have been imprisoned or killed. ]

In 1944, Plaszow prepared to deport its Jews to Auschwitz. Schindler petitioned the Germans to allow him to relocate his factory to the Sudetenland so that he could produce goods for the war effort. The German government agreed and ordered him to compile a list of workers that he needed to take with him. Schindler made a list of more than 1,000 Jews that he claimed were essential for his factory. The employees on the list were saved from being sent to Auschwitz and spared the horrors of camp life. They spent the remaining months of World War II in Schindler's factory.

---

**Non-violent resistance efforts included hiding Jews, listening to forbidden Allied radio broadcasts, and producing anti-Nazi newspapers.**

---

## BEAR WITNESS ✡

In Eastern Europe, if a person was caught helping or sheltering Jews, their entire family was sentenced to death.

# THE WHITE ROSE

Even within Germany, some people resisted the Nazis and their policies. In the summer of 1942, a group of young German people formed a resistance group called the White Rose. It was made up of students from the University of Munich and their professor. After witnessing the murder of Jews on the Eastern Front, the group authored six anti-Nazi leaflets, which called Germans to passively resist the Nazis.

> They painted slogans such as "Freedom!" and "Down With Hitler!" around the university.

In February 1943, the group's leaders, Hans and Sophie Scholl and Christoph Probst, were caught distributing their pamphlets. They were arrested and executed. Later that year, their professor advisor, Kurt Huber, and other student leaders associated with the White Rose were also executed. Just before his execution, Hans Scholl repeated the words of German author and philosopher Johann Wolfgang von Goethe, "Hold out in defiance of all despotism."

# PARTISAN FIGHTERS

Some Jews escaped the ghettos and formed guerilla-style fighting units. These fighters were called partisans—they hid and lived in the dense forests of Eastern Europe. In the Soviet Union, Czechoslovakia, Yugoslavia, Greece, and Poland, partisans planned quick attacks and sabotage on Nazi targets.

## REPRISALS

German reprisals against protestors were deadly. In Czechoslovakia, resistors fatally injured Reinhard Heydrich, the leading planner of Hitler's Final Solution. The two attackers escaped and hid in a Prague cathedral.

To avenge Heydrich's death, the Nazis ordered the execution of 10,000 Czechs. In a nearby village, where the assassins' radio transmitter was discovered, the Nazis killed every adult. They removed the children for reeducation in Germany.

A few days later, the Nazis gathered the residents of Lidice, a village outside Prague. Claiming that a member of the village had aided the assassins, the Nazis took groups of men and women behind a barn and shot them. The children were sent to concentration camps or Germany. Then, SS officers destroyed the town and removed its name from all official records.

Near the Lithuanian capital city of Vilna, a large group of partisans disrupted hundreds of Nazi trains and killed more than 3,000 German soldiers. In Belorussia, there were as many as 5,000 partisan fighters in 1941. Most of these fighters were Soviet troops cut off from the army and escaped prisoners of war. Some Jews who had escaped from the ghettos joined partisan units. In the Lithuanian forests, the Jews of Vilna organized about 400 fighters into four battalions.

Partisan life was difficult. Living in the forest, they had to constantly move from place to place, never staying in one area for too long. Partisans were always searching for food and shelter, often raiding local farms and villages for supplies. They built flimsy shelters that offered scant protection against the bitter winter weather.

> And partisans lived in constant fear that they would be discovered and captured by German troops.

Most of the partisan units consisted of unmarried, able-bodied men. Some units were unwilling to leave behind those who were unable to fight with them. These groups established a family camp, where women, children, and the elderly could live under the protection of the partisan fighters. As many as 10,000 Jews survived in partisan family camps.

## GHETTO UPRISINGS

Within the ghettos, some Jews resisted Nazi oppression with organized armed resistance. In April and May 1943, Jews in the Warsaw Ghetto revolted against the Germans. They had heard that the Germans were planning to deport the last of those living in the ghetto to the Treblinka killing center.

When the German SS and police entered the ghetto to begin the deportations, members of the Jewish Fighting Organization and other groups attacked. They threw homemade explosives and fired with small guns at the German tanks and soldiers.

The initial attacks stunned the German soldiers and forced them to retreat outside the ghetto. After fighting continued for a month, the Germans blew up Warsaw's Great Synagogue. This signaled the end of the uprising and the destruction of the ghetto. Any remaining ghetto inhabitants were deported. For months after the uprising, Jewish resistance fighters hid in the ghetto ruins and continued to attack the Germans.

The Warsaw Ghetto Uprising was the first and largest uprising against the Germans in occupied Europe. The bravery of the fighters inspired similar uprisings in other ghettos, such as Vilna, Bialystok, and Minsk, as well as uprisings in the Treblinka and Sobibor killing centers.

Scene from the Warsaw Ghetto Uprising

photo credit: National Archives

# WAR REFUGEE BOARD

The United States did not get officially involved in efforts to rescue Jews from the Holocaust until January 1944. Although the U.S. State Department received reports of mass murder as early as 1942, department officials did not act on the information. Instead, they insisted that the best way to help the Jewish people was to defeat Germany as quickly as possible.

In 1944, the Secretary of the Treasury Henry Morgenthau convinced President Franklin D. Roosevelt to create the War Refugee Board. It worked with Jewish organizations, diplomats, and resistance groups to help Jews escape Nazi-occupied areas. They also provided relief to prisoners of Nazi concentration camps. One of the board's agents was Raoul Wallenberg, a Swedish diplomat in Budapest, Hungary. He helped tens of thousands of Jews in Hungary by giving them protective Swedish passports, which prevented them from being deported to Auschwitz. Wallenberg also helped to set up hospitals and soup kitchens for Hungarian Jews.

The War Refugee Board helped rescue as many as 200,000 Jews. However, many critics believe that many more could have been saved if the board had gotten involved earlier.

## BEAR WITNESS ✡

When the Soviets liberated Budapest, Raoul Wallenberg disappeared. He was last seen with Soviet troops in January 1945. Years later, the Soviet Union disclosed that Wallenberg was arrested and had died in prison in 1947.

## KEY QUESTIONS

- Why did some people ignore the Holocaust while others put themselves at risk to help people escape death and mistreatment?

- How might World War II and the Holocaust have been different if resistors had managed to assassinate Hitler? Would the Nazi Party have remained as strong?

- What can you do to help people who are being persecuted today?

# RIGHTEOUS AMONG THE NATIONS

In 1953, Yad Vashem was established in Jerusalem as the world's center for documentation, research, education, and commemoration of the Holocaust. In documenting the story of the Holocaust, Yad Vashem has recognized a group of people known as "Righteous Among the Nations." These people are non-Jews who risked their lives to save Jews during the Holocaust. These men and women came from all countries and backgrounds and their actions took many forms. Some provided shelter, while others assisted escape in some way. They all acted to save Jewish lives.

- **You can explore the Yad Vashem website here.** Learn more about the requirements to be honored as a Righteous Among the Nations. 🔍 Yad Vashem

- **Explore stories of individual members of this group here.**  Yad Vashem Righteous Among Nations list

- **Select a member of the Righteous Among the Nations to research.** Write an essay, prepare a speech, or create a presentation to justify their selection using the Yad Vashem criteria.

  - What did they do during the Holocaust?

  - How did they risk their life to save others?

  - What was their motivation?

  - Why was this person selected for the honor of being designated a Righteous Among the Nations?

To investigate more, create a poem or piece of art that expresses what you have learned about what it means to be Righteous Among the Nations.

# TYPES OF RESISTANCE

After the Holocaust, many people asked why the Jews did not fight back. In fact, it is not true that they did not fight back. Jewish people living under Nazi rule resisted in many ways, each using the opportunities available to him or her. There are two main types of resistance—active and passive.

Active resistance is doing something to interfere with the enemy's goals or operations. In contrast, passive resistance is refusing to act and not doing something that the enemy wants.

Both types of resistance can be direct, which means it's carried out against the enemy, or indirect, which means it's carried out to support an oppressed person or community. Many acts of resistance fit into more than one category.

- **Brainstorm a list of resistance activities that you could do if you were living in one of the Nazi ghettos.**

  - Think about what resistance really is and how it applied to the Holocaust.

  - What goals to you hope to accomplish with your resistance activities?

To investigate more, create a chart and organize your resistance activities. Group the activities according to whether they are active or passive and direct or indirect. Present your findings to classmates, friends, and family.

# Chapter 8 ▶
# The Legacy of the Holocaust

Is genocide still a problem we need to be wary of in today's world?

**STUDYING THE HOLOCAUST HAS BEEN INTENSE, BUT I'VE LEARNED A LOT.**

**ME, TOO. I ALSO LEARNED SOMETHING THAT I DIDN'T EXPECT.**

**YEAH? LIKE WHAT?**

**THAT THE HOLOCAUST DIDN'T BEGIN IN THE GAS CHAMBERS...**

**...IT BEGAN WITH WORDS.**

While the Holocaust remains the worst example of a mass killing, people still find reasons to commit genocide against other groups.

The Holocaust ended in 1945 with the end of Word War II, but its effects are still felt around the world today. In the following years, there have been attempts to compensate victims and bring war criminals to justice. By learning about the events that led up to and were part of the Holocaust, we hope to stop genocide from happening.

The horrors discovered at the killing centers outraged citizens and politicians around the world. Once the war was over, the Allied leaders, including President Franklin D. Roosevelt of the United States, Prime Minister Winston Churchill of Great Britain, and General Secretary Joseph Stalin of the Soviet Union, declared that they would bring the Nazi leaders to justice.

The Allies decided to conduct trials at Nuremberg, one of the few German cities that was not in ruins from the war. The trials of leading German officials before the International Military Tribunal opened on November 20, 1945.

# THE NUREMBERG TRIALS

The United States, Great Britain, the Soviet Union, and France each supplied a judge and a prosecution team. These were 24 Nazi leaders who were charged with crimes against peace, war crimes, crimes against humanity, and conspiracy. Of these men, 22 stood trial in Nuremberg. They included Nazi Party officials, key cabinet officials, military leaders, and the ministers of armaments and labor. At the trials, testimony revealed the details of the Holocaust, including the Auschwitz death camp, the destruction of the Warsaw Ghetto, the estimated 6 million Jewish victims, and 5 million Romani, homosexual, and other non-Jewish victims.

On October 1, 1946, the judges sentenced Hermann Göring, the highest-ranking Nazi official, and 11 other men to death by hanging. Göring escaped execution by committing suicide. The remaining men were hanged and cremated in Dachau. Seven defendants were sentenced to prison, while three were acquitted.

During the next few years, additional trials were held to prosecute those responsible for the deaths of millions of people in concentration camps throughout German-occupied Europe. These trials prosecuted concentration camp guards, police officers, members of the Einsatzgruppen mobile killing units, and doctors who performed medical experiments.

Even top executives of Germany companies that used Jewish slave labor and supplied the Zyklon B for the gas chambers were put on trial. These war criminals were tried by military courts in occupied Germany and Austria. Some war criminals were tried in the courts of the countries where they had committed their crimes.

## BEAR WITNESS ✡

The International Military Tribunal defined crimes against humanity as "murder, extermination, enslavement, deportation . . . or persecutions on political, racial, or religious grounds."

## THE NUREMBERG CODE

During the trial of Nazi doctors, the U.S. military tribunal issued guidelines on the use of human subjects in medical experiments. These guidelines became known as the Nuremberg Code. They formed the foundation of today's medical ethics and the right of the patient to "informed consent."

Defendants during the Nuremberg trials

photo credit: National Archives

## TRIAL OF ADOLF EICHMANN

Adolf Eichmann, the head of the Gestapo's section for Jewish affairs, planned and organized deportations to Nazi death camps. He also ordered the seizure of property from deported Jews. After the war, Eichmann fled to Argentina, where he started a new life under the name Ricardo Klement. In 1960, Israeli agents discovered Eichmann and he was charged with crimes against the Jewish people and against humanity. Many Holocaust survivors testified at Eichmann's trial. He was found guilty, and on June 1, 1962, Eichmann was executed by hanging.

For the first time in history, leaders of a regime were held legally accountable for the crimes committed by its citizens as they carried out government policies. Individuals were held accountable for their actions. They were not able to hide behind the excuse that they were following orders from a superior.

The Nuremberg trials brought only a small number of Nazi war criminals to justice. Many who participated in the crimes against Jews and others escaped justice. Some simply resumed their pre-war lives. Others adopted new identities in Germany, South America, or the Middle East. Thousands of war criminals entered the United States pretending to be anti-communists fleeing Soviet persecution. The U.S. government itself moved some Nazi war criminals to the United States as part of Operation Paperclip, which brought 1,600 of the best German and Austrian scientists to the United States to work for the military and National Aeronautics and Space Administration.

In 1979, the United States Department of Justice established an Office of Special Investigation to hunt down Nazi war criminals hiding in the United States. In the following years, the office opened hundreds of investigations into suspected Nazi war criminals.

# COMPENSATION FOR VICTIMS

When the Nazis deported the Jews to concentration camps, they confiscated their personal property. After the Holocaust, survivors and organizations attempted to receive payment from Germany, other governments, banks, and industries for the stolen valuables.

Although many people killed in the Holocaust had bank accounts in Switzerland, the banks refused to release the accounts to relatives without the proper paperwork. Because there were no death certificates for those murdered by the Nazis, many did not have the necessary documents. In addition, bank documents were lost when families were thrown out of their homes and their personal belongings were confiscated. After pressure to release the money, the Swiss banks donated funds to charity. In 1997, they finally allowed survivors to access bank records.

# THE UNITED NATIONS

From August to October 1944, representatives from China, the Soviet Union, Great Britain, and the United States met to discuss forming a new international organization to promote cooperation between countries and stop future wars. In 1945, representatives from 50 countries attended the United Nations Conference on International Organization. They established the United Nations (UN) on October 24, 1945.

During the next three years, the UN adopted several agreements, including the Convention on the Prevention and Punishment of the Crime of Genocide in 1948. The genocide convention was designed in response to the defendants at Nuremberg who claimed they had violated no laws.

*The international community agreed that war could not be used as an excuse to commit crimes against humans.*

## UNIVERSAL DECLARATION OF HUMAN RIGHTS

You can read the document here. Is there anything you would add to or subtract from this document if you were helping to draft it? Do you think this document has made a difference in how people are treated around the world since it was written in 1948?

🔎 Universal Declaration of Human Rights

Article 2 of the convention defines genocide as "any of the following acts committed with intent to destroy, in whole or in part, a national, ethnic, racial, or religious group." The acts of genocide include the following.

- Killing members of a group

- Causing serious bodily or mental harm to members of a group

- Purposely inflicting living conditions on a group that could cause complete or partial extermination

- Enforcing measures to prevent births in a group

- Removing children from one group by force and transferring them to another group

On December 10, 1948, the UN adopted the Universal Declaration of Human Rights (UDHR). For the first time in history, the international community agreed that serious violations of human rights should not be tolerated. They acknowledged that protecting human rights was not the responsibility of one single country, but was the responsibility of the entire world.

Eleanor Roosevelt, First Lady and human rights activist, holds the Universal Declaration of Human Rights.

photo credit: National Archives

The UDHR lists the fundamental human rights that are to be universally protected. All member countries were called upon to publicize the UDHR so that it could be shared, displayed, read, and discussed around the world.

# PRESENT AND FUTURE

Despite the tragic experience of the Holocaust, genocide keeps happening. In 1994, rivalry between the Hutu and Tutsi ethnic groups in Rwanda led to genocide. During a period of 100 days, state-sponsored violence led to the murder of 800,000 Tutsi and their supporters. Hutu paramilitary groups planned and carried out the attacks.

Other examples of genocide include the Cambodia Killing Fields between 1975 to 1979 and the war in Darfur, Sudan, which began in 2003, during which hundreds of thousands of Darfur's non-Arab population were killed. The human race continues to inflict violence upon itself, despite the lessons from history. How can we do better?

The Holocaust was one of the greatest tragedies in human history. By remembering the victims, honoring the survivors, and learning how the Holocaust began and how it evolved, many people believe that there is hope for the future.

## THE WORLD MUST NOT FORGET

The genocide committed by Nazi Germany stunned the world. After the war ended, when other countries realized the scale on which atrocities had been committed in German-occupied lands, people understood it was important to remember what had happened. Remembering might help to keep it from happening again. You can read a news article from 1945 that describes what one person saw in the camps.

New York Times must not forget

## KEY QUESTIONS

- What can you learn about intolerance and racism from the global refugee crisis happening today?
- What can you learn about genocide that is happening today?
- What can you do to keep genocide from happening?

## VOCAB LAB

Write down what you think each of the following words means. What root words can you find for help?

**compensate**, **crimes against humanity**, **acquit**, **Operation Paperclip**, **conspiracy**, **justice**, and **war criminal**.

Compare your definitions with those of your friends or classmates. Did you all come up with the same meanings? Turn to the text and glossary if you need help.

To investigate more, research another genocide in recent history. What events led to the violence? How did the international community respond? What actions if any could have prevented the genocide?

# CREATE A PLEDGE TO PREVENT GENOCIDE

Genocide does not occur by itself. It is the result of people, organizations, and governments making choices to allow discrimination, prejudice, and hatred of certain groups of people based on religion, nationality, or ethnicity. Although the United Nations declared genocide an international crime in 1948, it still exists today in many parts of the world. People in Yugoslavia, Rwanda, the Sudan, and Syria have been targets of genocide.

- **Think about how the lessons of the Holocaust can help people today fight genocide.** Think about how genocide affects your own life. Consider the following questions.

  - What is the international community? Are you a part of it?

  - What role does the international community play during genocide?

  - Does the international community have the responsibility to assist countries threatened by genocide?

  - What role can average citizens play in assisting when genocide threatens?

  - How can students get involved to prevent genocide?

- **Create a pledge to prevent genocide.** Include specific actions that you can do.

# CREATE A HOLOCAUST MEMORIAL

In the years since the Holocaust, many memorials have been built to remember the Holocaust and its victims. Some memorials display Holocaust artifacts, while others feature sculpture and art to express feelings. Some art expresses pain and grief, while others focus on new life and hope.

- **In Berlin, the Memorial to the Murdered Jews of Europe is a large area covered with 2,711 concrete slabs arranged in a grid pattern.** The design represents an ordered system that has lost touch with human reason. Visitors can reflect as they walk between the slabs. An information center holds historical film, photos, and video interviews with survivors to educate visitors to the memorial. You can view a gallery of Holocaust memorials here.

  🔍 Florida Center teacher guide Holocaust

- **Using what you have learned about the Holocaust, design and create a memorial to the Holocaust, its victims, and survivors.** Consider the following in your design.

  - What form will you use?

  - Who is your intended audience?

  - What message or feeling are you trying to convey?

  - Will you use symbols in your memorial? What will they represent?

- **Share your memorial with classmates, friends, and family.** See if they can guess the meaning and message behind the memorial.

> To investigate more, create a visitor's guide for your memorial. What information is important to understand the background and meaning of the memorial? How will you share that information with visitors?

## BEAR WITNESS ✡

In January 2000, representatives from 44 nations met in Stockholm, Sweden, to talk about the importance of Holocaust education, remembrance, and research. Many governments established an annual Holocaust Memorial Day. In 2005, the United Nations marked January 27th as International Holocaust Remembrance Day, which is the anniversary of the liberation of the Auschwitz-Birkenau death camp by the Soviet army in 1945.

# PREJUDICE AND HUMAN RIGHTS IN THE NEWS

The UDHR states that certain human rights are universally protected. By searching through a recent newspaper, we can see how human rights are still being violated and how discrimination and racism still exist throughout the world.

- **Search through several newspapers and magazines to find articles, editorials, advertisements, and other features that deal with human rights, discrimination, and racism.** Select an article that discusses genocide or discrimination.

  - How does the event and information in the article compare to what you have learned about the Holocaust?

  - In what ways are they similar? What differences exist?

  - Are there any bystanders who have stepped forward to help? Why or why not?

To investigate more, think of works of fiction that portray different issues about discrimination, racism, and genocide. Have you seen movies, read books, or listened to music that highlights a struggle for human rights? How is the impact of fiction different from the impact of nonfiction? Why are both genres valuable?

**abdicate:** to give up or renounce one's throne.

**abstract:** existing more in thought and ideas than in reality.

**acquit:** to find someone not guilty of a criminal charge.

**alliance:** a partnership formed for mutual benefit, especially between countries or organizations.

**Allies:** an alliance between Great Britain, the United States, and the Soviet Union during World War II.

**ambassador:** the head diplomat who represents the government of one country in dealings with another country or organization.

**animosity:** strong hostility.

**annex:** to incorporate territory into a country.

**anti-Semitism:** hostility toward people who practice Judaism.

**armistice:** an agreement or truce between opposing sides in a war to stop fighting.

**Aryan:** in Nazi doctrine, a non-Jewish Caucasian person.

**assassination:** to kill someone.

**asset:** something useful or valuable.

**asylum:** the protection granted by a nation to someone who has left their native country as a political refugee.

**atrocity:** a cruel act of violence.

**autobiographical:** a story told about oneself.

**Axis:** an alliance between Germany, Italy, and Japan during World War II.

**barracks:** a building or group of buildings used to house soldiers.

**battalion:** a large body of troops ready for battle.

**boycott:** avoiding a business or an organization as a form of punishment or protest.

**broadcast:** to transmit by radio or television.

**brutality:** great physical and mental cruelty.

**cabinet:** senior members of the government who advise the chief executive.

**casualty:** a person who is injured or killed during war.

**chancellor:** the head of government in some countries.

**charismatic:** having a charming nature that inspires devotion in others.

**citizen:** a person who legally belongs to a country and has the rights and protection of that country.

**civil rights:** the rights that every person should have, regardless of his or her gender, race, or religion.

**collaborate:** to work together.

**commemoration:** remembrance, typically expressed in a ceremony.

**communism:** a system of government in which everything is owned and run by the government.

**compensate:** to give something, usually money, in recognition of loss, suffering, or injury incurred.

**concentration camp:** during World War II, large camps where Jews and members of other groups were imprisoned by the Nazis and forced to perform hard labor or exterminated.

**conscript:** to enlist someone into the armed forces involuntarily.

**conspiracy:** a secret plan by a group to do something unlawful or harmful.

**consulate:** the place or building in which an ambassador's duties are carried out.

**contagious:** easy to catch.

**coup:** a sudden, violent, and illegal seizure of power from a government.

**crematorium:** a place where a dead person's body is burned or cremated.

**crimes against humanity:** certain acts that are deliberately committed as part of a widespread or systematic attack directed against any civilian population or an identifiable part of a population.

**crucifixion:** the execution of a person by nailing them to a cross.

**culture:** the beliefs and way of life of a group of people, which can include religion, language, art, clothing, food, holidays, and more.

**curfew:** a regulation requiring people to remain indoors between specified hours, typically at night.

# GLOSSARY

**death march:** a forced march of prisoners of war or other captives or deportees with the intent to kill, brutalize, weaken, or demoralize as many of the captives as possible along the way.

**delegate:** a person sent or authorized to represent others, in particular an elected representative sent to a conference.

**delouse:** to rid a person of lice and other insects.

**democracy:** a system of government elected freely by the people.

**deport:** to expel a person from a country.

**despotism:** the exercise of absolute power, especially in a cruel and oppressive way.

**dictatorship:** a government by a dictator with absolute rule over the people.

**diplomat:** a person sent by the government to deal with another country.

**discrimination:** the unfair treatment of a person or a group of people because of their identity.

**disembark:** to get off a ship or airplane.

**displaced person:** a person who is forced to leave their home country because of war, persecution, or natural disaster. A refugee.

**divert:** to change course or turn from one direction to another.

**domination:** to exercise control over someone or something.

**economy:** a system of producing and consuming goods and services.

**efficient:** wasting as little time as possible in completing a task.

**Einsatzgruppen:** Nazi mobile killing units generally made up of German SS and police personnel.

**elite:** a small group of powerful people.

**emigrant:** a person who leaves their own country to settle in another country.

**emigrate:** to leave one's own country in order to settle permanently in another.

**Enabling Act:** a 1933 Weimar Constitution amendment that gave the German cabinet the power to enact laws without the involvement of the Reichstag.

**ethnic:** a group of people of the same race or nationality who share a distinctive culture.

**euthanasia:** the killing of a patient suffering from an incurable and painful disease or in an irreversible coma.

**evacuate:** to move a person from one place to another as a protective measure.

**exaggeration:** to make something sound larger, greater, better, or worse than it really is.

**exile:** to expel someone from their native country as a punishment.

**expel:** to drive or push out.

**exposure:** being unprotected from the extremes of the outdoors, such as the cold and snow or the heat and sun.

**exterminate:** to destroy completely.

**eyewitness:** a person who sees an act or event and can give a firsthand account of it.

**fascists:** followers of fascism, a form of radical, authoritarian nationalism.

**fiction:** stories that describe imaginary events and people.

**Final Solution:** the Nazi policy of murdering all the European Jews.

**folklore:** the traditional beliefs, customs, and stories of a community, passed through the generations by word of mouth.

**front:** the dividing point where two armies meet.

**führer:** a leader with the unlimited powers of a dictator.

**gas chamber:** a sealed room used for killing people or animals with poison gas.

**genocide:** destroying a racial, political, or cultural group or the language, religion, or culture of a group.

**Gestapo:** the secret police of Nazi Germany under the control of the SS.

**ghetto:** a section of a city inhabited by one minority group.

**Great Depression:** the deepest and longest-lasting economic downturn in the history of the Western industrialized world. The Great Depression occurred between 1929 and 1939.

**guerilla:** a member of a small independent group taking part in irregular fighting, typically against larger regular forces.

**haven:** a place that is safe and protected.

**Holocaust:** a time before and during World War II when the German Nazis tried to kill the entire Jewish race, as well as several other groups.

**homosexual:** a person who is sexually attracted to others of the same gender.

**hostage:** a person held against their will by another person or group in order to ensure demands are met.

**hostile:** very unfriendly, relating to an enemy.

**human rights:** the rights that belong to all people, such as freedom from torture, the right to live, and freedom from slavery.

**humane:** treating a living creature with compassion.

**humanitarian:** having to do with helping the welfare or happiness of people.

**hygiene:** practices that keep things clean and prevent the spread of germs.

**ideology:** a system of ideas and ideals, especially one that forms the basis of economic or political theory and policy.

**illustrative:** a clear, realistic example.

**immigrant:** a person who moves to a country to live permanently.

**immigration:** moving to a new country to live there.

**impersonal:** not influenced by, showing, or involving personal feelings.

**impressionist:** a way of painting that conveys emotion, mood, and impression rather than an objective reality.

**irony:** for humor or emphasis, expressing a meaning by using language that says the opposite.

**justice:** fair treatment.

**labeling:** judging someone or something by describing them or it in a certain way.

**inferior:** of a lesser quality, status, or rank.

**inflation:** a general increase in prices that results in a fall in the purchasing value of money.

**instability:** not dependable or steady.

**institution:** a society or organization founded for a religious, educational, or social, purpose, or an established law, practice, or custom.

**internment camp:** a prison or detention camp used during wartime.

**intolerance:** the unwillingness to accept beliefs and behaviors different from one's own.

**invalidate:** to make something not legal or official.

**Islam:** a religion developed in the Middle East that follows the teachings of the prophet Muhammad.

**isolationist:** someone who follows a policy of remaining apart from and uninvolved with the politics of other countries.

**Jew:** a person whose religion is Judaism.

**Judaism:** a religion that uses the Torah as its sacred text.

**Judenrat:** a Jewish council created under German orders that was responsible for internal matters in a ghetto.

**kaiser:** a German or Austrian emperor.

**Kindertransport:** a series of rescue efforts that brought thousands of refugee Jewish children to Great Britain from Nazi Germany between 1938 and 1940.

**Kristallnacht:** the wave of violent anti-Jewish pogroms that took place on November 9 and 10, 1938, in Germany.

**liberate:** to set someone free, especially from slavery or imprisonment.

**literal:** representing something as it is, without exaggeration or embellishment.

**Luftwaffe:** the German air force during World War II.

**maltreatment:** cruel or violent treatment of a person.

**mass murder:** the murder of a large number of people.

**medieval:** describes the Middle Ages, the period of European history after the fall of the Roman Empire, from about 350 to 1450.

**messiah:** a promised savior and deliverer.

**millennium:** 1,000 years. Plural is millennia.

**minority:** a part of the population that is different or is a smaller group.

**moderate:** not following extreme views, especially in politics.

**morale:** the confidence and enthusiasm of a person or group.

**morality:** the distinction between right and wrong or good and bad behavior.

**Muslim:** a person who follows the religion of Islam.

# GLOSSARY

**nationalism:** devotion or loyalty to one's country; patriotism.

**nationalism:** loyalty and devotion to one's country.

**Nazi:** the main political party of Germany before and during World War II.

**nonfiction:** writing that is based on facts, real events, and real people.

**Nuremberg Laws:** anti-Jewish laws enacted by Germany on September 15, 1935.

**occupy:** to take control of an area or country by military conquest or settlement.

**offensive:** an attacking military campaign.

**Operation Paperclip:** a program in which more than 1,600 German scientists, engineers, and technicians were recruited and brought to the United States for government employment from post-Nazi Germany.

**oppress:** to use unjust or cruel authority and power to persecute someone.

**optimistic:** hopeful and confident about the future or how something will work out.

**paramilitary:** a military group or organization that is not part of a country's armed forces.

**parliamentary democracy:** a form of government where voters elect the members of parliament and a chancellor or prime minister then forms the government.

**partisan:** a member of a party of light or irregular troops engaged in harassing an enemy.

**perceive:** to become aware of something.

**persecution:** a campaign to exterminate or drive away a group of people based on their religious beliefs or other characteristic.

**pessimistic:** gloomy or negative about the future or how something will work out.

**pogrom:** an organized massacre of a particular group.

**prejudice:** a preconceived opinion or judgment about someone that is not based on reason or actual experience.

**prevail:** to prove to be more powerful, to be victorious.

**propaganda:** information, especially of a biased or misleading nature, that is used to promote or publicize a particular political cause or point of view.

**prophetic:** accurately describing what will happen in the future.

**prosecute:** to conduct legal proceedings against someone charged with a crime.

**quota:** a limit on the number of people or objects.

**race:** a group of people that shares distinct physical qualities, such as skin color.

**racism:** to believe that all members of a race possess certain traits and to judge these traits as inferior to one's own. Negative opinions or treatment of people based on race.

**rally:** a large gathering of people to show support for a cause or to protest.

**rationalize:** to explain or justify behavior or actions based on reasons that may or may not be true.

**recruit:** to enlist someone into the armed forces.

**reeducation:** attempts to instill certain beliefs into people.

**refugee center:** a place where people who have lost their homes due to war or a natural disaster can go for shelter, food, and other assistance.

**regime:** a government or system, especially one that has firm control over people.

**register:** to enter or record on an official list.

**reparation:** to make amends for something, often by paying money.

**reprieve:** the cancellation or postponement of a punishment.

**reprisal:** an act of retaliation.

**resilience:** the ability to recover quickly from setbacks.

**resistance:** a force that opposes or slows down another force.

**restraint:** to hold back and keep under control.

**resurgence:** an increase or revival after a period of little activity, popularity, or occurrence.

**resurrection:** the rising of Jesus from the dead in Christianity.

**retribution:** a punishment inflicted on someone as vengeance.

**rights:** what is due to a person naturally or legally.

**riot:** a gathering of people protesting something that gets out of control and violent.

**Romani:** a member of a group of people in Europe living a nomadic life, moving from place to place.

**ruthlessness:** having no pity for other people.

**SA:** stands for Sturmabteilung (stormtroopers). The original paramilitary arm of the Nazi party, known as the brownshirts, it lost power to the SS in 1934 in an event known as the Night of the Long Knives.

**sabotage:** the planned destruction of property, or an act that interferes with work or another activity.

**scapegoat:** someone or something blamed for a failure.

**sedative:** a substance or drug that has a relaxing effect.

**segregate:** to separate or divide people based on race, religion, or class.

**shtetl:** a small Jewish town or village formerly found in Eastern Europe.

**smuggle:** to move goods secretly or illegally.

**Sonderkommando:** work units made up of German Nazi death camp prisoners.

**SS:** stands for Schutzstaffel (Protection Squadron), a paramilitary arm of the Nazi party. The SS carried out surveillance and terror within Germany and German-occupied Europe and was responsible for implementing the genocide of the Holocaust.

**State of Israel:** a Jewish state in the Middle East created after World War II, settled by many European Jews.

**steadfast:** firm and unwavering.

**superior:** higher in rank, status, or quality.

**suspension:** to stop something temporarily.

**swastika:** a Nazi symbol that looks like a hooked cross.

**symbol:** an image that stands for something else.

**symbolism:** the use of symbols to represent ideas or qualities.

**synagogue:** a building used for Jewish religious services.

**systematic:** done according to a plan.

**tolerance:** the willingness to respect or accept behavior and beliefs that are different from your own.

**trade guild:** an organization established to protect people who are in a certain business or trade.

**transit camp:** a holding place for Jews, before they are sent to concentration camps, labor camps, or death camps.

**treason:** the crime of betraying one's country.

**treaty:** a formal agreement between countries.

**Treaty of Versailles:** a peace treaty signed in 1919 that ended World War I. It forced Germany to take responsibility for the war and to pay reparations.

**trial:** a formal examination of evidence before a judge and jury.

**trusts:** an agreement in which property and assets are held by one person for the benefit of another person.

**tyrant:** a cruel ruler who denies people their rights.

**unemployment:** the state of joblessness.

**visa:** a document that allows the holder to enter, leave, or stay for a specific period of time in a country.

**war crime:** an action carried out during war that accepted international rules of war do not allow.

**Weimar Republic:** describes the government of Germany between 1919 and 1933.

**Zegota:** an underground organization of Polish resistance in German-occupied Poland.

# RESOURCES

## BOOKS

Bauer, Yehuda. *A History of the Holocaust*. Danbury, CT: Franklin Watts, 2001.

Berenbaum, Michael. *The World Must Know: The History of the Holocaust as Told in the United States Holocaust Memorial Museum*. Washington, DC: United States Holocaust Memorial Museum, 2005.

Bitton-Jackson, Livia. *I Have Lived a Thousand Years: Growing Up in the Holocaust*. New York: Simon & Schuster, 1997.

Larson, Erik. *In the Garden of Beasts: Love, Terror, and an American Family in Hitler's Berlin*. New York: Random House Inc., 2011.

Opdyke, Irene Gut. *In My Hands: Memories of a Holocaust Rescuer*. New York: Ember, 2016.

Steele, Philip. *The Holocaust: The Origins, Events, and Remarkable Tales of Survival*. New York: Scholastic, 2016.

Wood, Angela Gluck. *Holocaust: The Events and Their Impact on Real People*. New York: DK, 2015.

## MUSEUMS

Auschwitz-Birkenau Memorial and Museum, Oświęcim, Poland: auschwitz.org

Holocaust Museum Houston, Houston, TX: hmh.org

Los Angeles Museum of the Holocaust, Los Angeles, CA: lamoth.org

United States Holocaust Memorial Museum, Washington, DC: ushmm.org

Yad Vashem: The World Holocaust Remembrance Center, Jerusalem, Israel: yadvashem.org

## WEBSITES

**ushmm.org/learn/students/the-holocaust-a-learning-site-for-students**
The Holocaust: A Learning Site for Students

**theholocaustexplained.org**
The Holocaust Explained

**jewishvirtuallibrary.org/jsource/Holocaust/history.html**
The Holocaust: The Jewish Virtual Library

# RESOURCES

## QR CODE GLOSSARY

**Page 8:** fcit.usf.edu/Holocaust/resource/gallery/FWALL.htm

**Page 8:** fcit.usf.edu/Holocaust/resource/gallery/ghetart.htm

**Page 8:** jewishgen.org/ForgottenCamps/Exhib/DrawEng.html

**Page 8:** english.illinois.edu/maps/holocaust/art.htm

**Page 9:** jhm.nl/collection/specials/charlotte-salomon

**Page 23:** youtube.com/watch?v=AHHr2SNjbnc

**Page 30:** germanhistorydocs.ghi-dc.org/sub_document.cfm?document_id=1496

**Page 32:** youtube.com/watch?v=PRkeahelZHM

**Page 36:** ushmm.org/propaganda/exhibit.html#/gallery

**Page 36:** ushmm.org/wlc/en/gallery.php?ModuleId=10005202&MediaType=ph

**Page 36:** research.calvin.edu/german-propaganda-archive/ww2era.htm

**Page 36:** bbc.co.uk/history/worldwars/wwtwo/nazi_propaganda_gallery.shtml

**Page 37:** ushmm.org/wlc/en/media_oi.php?ModuleId=0&MediaId=1143

**Page 50:** yadvashem.org/odot_pdf/Microsoft%20Word%20-%203118.pdf

**Page 50:** yadvashem.org/odot_pdf/Microsoft%20Word%20-%203696.pdf

**Page 50:** yadvashem.org/odot_pdf/Microsoft%20Word%20-%203702.pdf

**Page 50:** yadvashem.org/odot_pdf/Microsoft%20Word%20-%203726.pdf

**Page 50:** ushmm.org/wlc/en/media_ph.php?ModuleId=10005059&MediaId=950

**Page 62:** hmd.org.uk/resources/poetry

**Page 67:** yadvashem.org/odot_pdf/Microsoft%20Word%20-%203927.pdf

**Page 67:** yadvashem.org/odot_pdf/Microsoft%20Word%20-%203698.pdf

**Page 82:** bhcourier.com/retracing-ss-st-louis-history-survivors-story

**Page 82:** ushmm.org/online/st-louis/list.php

**Page 95:** yadvashem.org/yv/en/holocaust/resource_center/item.asp?gate=1-10

**Page 95:** yadvashem.org/righteous/stories

**Page 102:** un.org/en/universal-declaration-human-rights

**Page 103:** nytimes.com/learning/teachers/archival/19450506notforget.pdf

**Page 105:** fcit.usf.edu/holocaust/resource/gallery/gallery6.htm

# INDEX

# INDEX

# INDEX

# INDEX